Praise for Conquer Trauma Drama: Get Your Life Back

"This is a powerful journey that takes the reader from merely entertaining the idea of being a survivor to firmly establishing that it's not merely entertainment, but entirely possible to be a survivor, and all because of the didactic and experiential lessons sequentially outlined by Jo Standing in order to ignite healing within!"
Dr. Faith Brown | Author of *Burnout: The Gift*

"Jo Standing shows you how to recover and heal from trauma in this book. She uses tools and techniques that guarantee success. A trauma survivor herself, she will teach you how to overcome your fears and discover your inner strength and courage. Jo's vitality and life force come through as she addresses this serious issue with warmth and compassion."
Dr. Karyne Wilner | *Director, Core Energetics Academy, Professor Salve Regina University*

"This book is written with deep awareness and compassion. It is a gift for yourself *and anyone* you know that may need positive encouragement along the way . . . It will help you find clarity in the struggle!"
Julie Christopher | CEO of Biztuition, Intuitive Business Coach, Bestselling Author and Speaker

"Jo is an amazing person, true to herself and life. Her story is as inspirational and heartfelt as they come. She is a shining example of how to overcome as she sucks the marrow out of life itself."
Michael Hodge | Former United States Marine Corps, Quantico-trained, Veteran

"If you ever wonder what your fears can do for you then it's a stellar idea to read this book. Many of us drown in our sorrows but that same pain can be the reason why you strive forward. This book is a demonstration of that!"
Norman McKenzie | Los Angeles-based Actor as seen in the Netflix show *Love*

"This is a powerful book on discovering your inner-strength and the beauty within that can be lost due to trauma or the everyday stresses of life."
Wynn Westmoreland | Emmy-Award Winning Journalist

"The book is easy-to-read and offers amazing techniques to overcome our mental struggles. It's well-written and I think it's very useful not only for people who suffered trauma, but for people who want to help others who suffered it and, in my case, I haven't had anything serious, still, this book has great insights on how to be in charge of our emotions."
Alba Alamillo | Author of *The Dark Side of The Mind*

"A must read for anyone struggling to reclaim their body, and life, after any stressful or tragic event. The book is practical, easy-to-understand, and gives you effective ways to get your life back on track. Standing offers profound insight with practical ways to move beyond trauma as you work through the workbook that accompanies the book."
Dr. Felicia Clark | Author of *I Like My Body: A 52 Week Journal to Honor and Appreciate My Body*

"Being addicted to drama is no different than other substances. It limits your joy! Jo provides a clear message of hope and healing. With this book learn how to turn your coping methods into pillars of strengths. This book is a great starting place."
Renee Baribeau | Author of *The Winds of Spirit*, Hay House Publication

"Standing tells her story of healing after trauma and shares her passion to help others learn, grow and thrive! Her book is full of exercises and affirmations to assist the reader in merging the power of the mind, body and spirit to gradually conquer trauma drama. Whether you have experienced trauma or work with those who have, this book is a must read! I will recommend this to clients and colleagues!"
Cathy Ridgway | Hyde Park Craniosacral Therapist

"From both a scientific and experiential perspective, divorce, after the death of a close family member, is the most traumatic of everyday human experiences. I will be recommending Jo's book to my divorce mediation participants to help them recover from the trauma of their marital dissolution and to transform their lives from, as Jo would put it, divorce victim to healthy survivor!"

Tom DiGrazia | Author of *Light on Peacemaking: A Guide To Appropriate Dispute Resolution and Mediating Family Conflict*

"This book is a pleasantly cerebral explanation of the complicated feelings and crazy emotions that affect us after unthinkable events happen. These well-chosen words help to identify, understand, and clarify our inner confusion, so that we may somehow make sense of it all, in our own time."

Cat Dols | Author of *Get Your Goddess On*

"After reading this eye-opening book, I came to the realization that I wasn't going insane! I could see that everything I was experiencing was meant-to-be. Meaning, we are survivors by nature and we are wired for knowing trauma in our lives, as well as, depending on one's interpretation, even realizing trauma and its effects in order to become healthier than ever! But, here's the catch, this is only possible when we are intending to navigate towards a brighter future and toward the lives that we've always dreamed and known we are capable of living since we were trusting and fearless children."

Enrique L. Aguilar Valverde | First Sergeant United States Army (Ret.)

"More than a book. *Conquer Trauma Drama* is a support system. The way Standing shares her story and provides insight on how to reset your mind and open your heart back up to life, is truly valuable. Her story is heavy, but the way she relays it on the pages, feels as though you are in light conversation with the author. Use it as a tool to reconnect with

yourself or to understand loved ones who may be suffering from their own trauma drama."
Erika Cain | Performing Artist, Speaker

"Conquer Trauma Drama is a must read, and what I see as being the new reference in conquering and thriving after any type of real-life drama. It is well-written, and proposes simple strategies to get your life back. If you, or anyone you love suffers from trauma in any form this book can help you transform your life. Now, don't waste another second and get back to your life one step at a time!"
Luc Goulet, The Leverage Guy | Speaker and Author of *Leverage Your Mind: The Next Phase of Self-Empowerment*

Conquer
Trauma Drama

❧

Jo Standing

GET YOUR LIFE BACK

For additional enquiries, contact Jo Standing and Team at 1-844-IAM-VIVA and make sure to leave a voicemail at the prompt. Or, leave a message at the contact form located at the website's connect page at www.JoStanding.com.
To book the author to speak, lead workshops, classes, or programs with your business or not-for-profit contact the author directly at www.JoStanding.com.
Book Cover and 3D Art by Carol Pearl.
Library of Congress Control Number: 2015911104
ISBN 13: 9780692350652 (paperback)
ISBN: 0692350659

Copies of this book are given away for free by *The Viva Standing Foundation*, a government recognized 501(c)3. To learn more and donate visit www.VivaStanding.org.

"Our greatest glory is not in never falling, but in rising every time we fall." Confucius

Dedication

℘

I dedicate this book to the survivors of life's unwanted surprises.

Do you recognize that fruit is born from the ground up?

My unbound wish for you is that you learn from everything, and that people, in response, learn from you. May you be a survivor who is willing to shift, yet again. Once upon a time you knew yourself as a victim. Now, you see your shadow for what it is and you are born a *survivor*. Will you be bold and courageous enough to stand up and thrive now? Will you be daring enough to find movement in what was once your limitation? Might you be self-allowing enough to roll with life's enjoyments with full knowledge that joy itself is unlimited? You, *Survivor*, are my impetus to write this book.

I am so grateful for your being here on this page with me.

May we dig into these pages together with fervor, JOY, and the ability to flower yet once more in every area of life.

Introduction

༝

THIS BOOK IS TO HELP YOU navigate through the effects of trauma that are commonly known as PTSD. Over 7.7 million people suffer from PTSD at any given point in time. In 2015, the National Institutes of Health (NIH) acknowledged that you don't have to be physically hurt to have PTSD. An infographic published by *Mother Jones*, suggests that PTSD is far more common than physical wounds. The same news source quotes Robert Motta, Professor of Psychology at Hofstra University, as saying that post-trauma is a contagious disease because it also impacts the people who are closest to a person who is suffering.

Recognize Trauma reports that 60 percent of adults report experiencing abuse or other difficult family circumstances during childhood and 60 percent of youth age seventeen and younger have been exposed to crime, violence, and abuse either directly or indirectly. The National Trauma Institute tells us that each year trauma accounts for 41 million emergency department visits and 2.3 million hospital admissions across the nation. The Institute also reveals that it is because trauma is a disease that affects all ages of people, the life years lost to trauma are equal to the life years lost from cancer, heart disease, and HIV combined.

What many of us have not yet considered is the possibility that trauma may awaken otherwise dormant strength and self-realization, and might be an incredible driver for the exploration of otherwise unknown innate gifts within the survivor. Having experienced a trauma is not all bad or negative. Trauma not only grants us the opportunity to form a new community made of strong bonds and common ground, but to grow from *everything* we learn from being on our road to recovery.

An article in *Scientific American* talks about the possibility of specific types of trauma having surprisingly uplifting side effects on the survivor, such as illuminated intelligence or "savant-like" capabilities, otherwise unknown to the individual before the trauma.

In my personal experience, my right brain was awakened to new levels after what was the experience of physical, sexual, mental and emotional abuse. This led to me befriending and working alongside the local painters in the Santa Ynez Mountains near Santa Barbara, California, and months later, in the year 2003, finding my way into writing courses in Northern California, and later giving editorial feedback for a successful documentary in Hollywood. I contribute my right-brain awakening to the resistance I felt to the knowledge held within my logical mind. My subconscious took the facts of my earlier kidnapping and rape and told my mind that the event quite plainly did not happen and that it was unsafe to think of it as having happened. From my experience my logical self then instigated denial of the traumatic experience and my right brain went into overdrive.

So, how can we ignite new potential within ourselves in order to mobilize our lives after the frightening event of trauma?

What things can we do on a regular basis to maintain and sustain a positive state of being?

How can we see through attempts by others to make us *"right, again,"* when we may never be the exact people we were before the traumatic event(s)? It is, of course, important to feel out a heart of love in these other people and their real desire to see us happy. In fact, let us have empathy for those who see our happiness in the context of an old model of ourselves where we are 'meant' to be the *exact same* as we were before experiencing our life-changing event(s).

The keys and principles in this book will help you center yourself in a place of positive fear of where we would be if we were not to face ourselves as the people we are today, and the people we have perhaps unwillingly become due to the unexpected event(s). When we embrace our positive fear we learn what we are meant to do *and become* in the lives we are creating for ourselves today.

Although the people in our lives love us tremendously, even their outpourings of love cannot and will not help us until we *help ourselves* by making a choice every day to face how our traumas have affected us, and until we decide to make the appropriate changes in our lives in order to honor sensitive or "tender spots" left over from the initial pain of the trauma(s).

Thankfully, trauma can create heightened awareness of both ourselves and the world around us. The flip side of this is a condition of constant trepidation and anxiety known as *hypervigilance*. But you get to decide which idea you connect with more, associate with, and will play out in your daily life.

In the big picture, to be fully *awake* as a byproduct of having the unexpected happen—no matter how gruesome or frightening the event that caused your trauma may have been—is a life blessing!

On the days when you feel the whole world is sleeping to your pain, know that they may also be asleep to their own pain, too. It is absolutely nothing personal.

On this journey of healing I advise you to remember this: You and I, *we,* are the only two people who can help you and me. We must do work on ourselves *first* before we can have freedom again to live without being controlled by fear of the past, the unknown, or ourselves.

Now, may I suggest that you get yourself a nice cup of hot tea or coffee? And, then enjoy this adventure that is YOU, in full motion, on your healing journey.

It is a journey! Now, let's make it one!

My Chaos

As a prerequisite to writing this book I took classes at the Justice Institute of British Columbia in Vancouver, Canada, lived on a mountain eight hours from the city that is known for its healing powers for a summer, taught free classes in self-realization from my living room, frequented Esalen Institute in Northern California since 2003, journaled and explored my life extensively, and taught a *Trust, Risk, Fear* workshop at a men's transition home to newly-released convicts! Since my trauma occurred in the year 2002, I've continued to look for new ways to perceive life.

In hindsight, it is surprising to me that my students in the United States and Canada, for all these years, have never asked me what my reasons were for dedicating so much time to healing and empowerment through the holistic arts. Perhaps because of their ages, which were often double and triple my own, they had already seen enough of life to recognize that I knew enough of what I was talking about and so didn't feel the need to ask.

After all, we sense things about people. We can tell when they've gone through a lot and drawn wisdom from their experiences in order to come out on the other side, improved and complete within themselves.

Perhaps, it is not crucial even for you to know my reasons for being on this journey. However, I am going to give you an overview on this page of my life experiences to give context to some of where I am coming from as a person and as a writer. Nothing more, nothing less. As we will explore within this book, there is no room for feeling sorry for people because of their life experiences. If we feel sorry for them at all, it should be because of how they are *choosing* to respond to their life experiences in a manner that is of a disadvantage to themselves.

Remember, defeatists make their own beds.

So, out with my own traumatic experiences already. At eight years of age, my half-brother, my blood father's only son, was murdered. The murderer accounted putting the bullet into my brother's head 'because my brother and his lover had made a pass at him in their penthouse'. In other words, it was inadvertently blamed on the fact that my brother was a gay man. My father shut himself down after that. At my twelve years of age, he died, but was revived after five minutes of shock pads and given a pacemaker for his heart. When I was sixteen, he was finally laid to rest. The only person I would talk to for days after that was my boyfriend. At seventeen, when I was living in New York City, that boyfriend, also my sweet sixteen first, died on the floor of his prestigious college of a drug overdose. Only one week prior, I'd been raped. After the rape, I learned that the rapist, who was a silent partner in the restaurant where I worked, was in the Italian Mafia, as was everyone else around me much to my (naive) surprise.

At seventeen the above facts all piled up were a bit much for me to fathom.

I had the choice of a devout Catholic mother to turn to, high school friends whom I had been forced to leave behind the year prior, and had all but lost touch with, or sisters who despised me over typical family rivalry that is always present when parents' ability to give attention and time to their children is challenged due to parental illness.

The full deal with my New York kidnapping and rape is that I walked past a man sitting alone in the corner of the establishment where the company party was taking place and wondered what was wrong with him and if he was going to be okay. Later on, I discovered what was wrong with that man firsthand when he followed me outside the night-club to where I had been flagging a cab. That night, I put concern for this stranger over concern for myself. My upbringing taught me always to think of others *first*. My trauma as a young girl with a complicated family and the desire to heal us all led to the drama of my adolescence, teenage and even some of my adult years. Trauma led to drama that had I taken the time out to recognize the impact of my childhood traumas through self-observation, therapeutic practices, and working with a mentor I wouldn't have gone on to create more unlikely dramas in my teens and to encounter more uncalculated risk trauma.

That night of the rape I was asked if I wanted to ride in his cab since he would be driving the span of most of the town in order to get where he lived. I didn't want to ride with him and the cab driver who had pulled up to the curb, but due to my Southern upbringing I was worried about offending him or being rude by saying, "No thanks," to the ride share offer. Besides, what could possibly happen?

For whatever reason, the cab driver was no longer a neutral third party in the car. I got into the back whereas the rapist sat in the front. I told the driver that I lived off of 20th Street. Only when we passed by 20th and kept going, I spoke up, "Excuse me, sir, we missed my street."

The driver had nothing to say in reply. The rapist did, though. "Come to my place with me. It'll be fun."

"I don't want to go anywhere else tonight. I want to go home."

No response.

The cab sailed through every green light at 1 a.m., the back doors locked, ignorant of its actions.

Somewhere around West 67th Street, the cab stopped. Tommy the rapist exited the vehicle from the passenger side. Still not a peep from the driver. Did he have a gun held to him? Or had he been bought off to stay silent to my request to exit the cab that night? What was the cause of his blind indifference to another's freedom, anyway?

Tommy opened my door as the taxi cab driver pressed the electronic unlock button for him to do so.

I was grabbed by the arm. Led into the brownstone. Told to be quiet. To cooperate. To be still. Raped. And eventually, after the break of dawn, released.

How Do You Know if This Book is For You?

Trauma means many things, but for a moment we will focus on the traumatic experience of rape. Maybe you've experienced a rape yourself or, if not, you've without a doubt at least heard the word *rape* and knew from the sound of it that it was a horrible and unspeakable thing to experience in one's life. Maybe you heard of a neighbor who was raped, or have a family member, friend, classmate, or colleague who has sadly experienced the whole-being violation of rape itself. If this is the case, upon hearing about your peer's experience you may have even explored what that rape means to you. Or what it means to the individual you know who has lived the experience. Perhaps you've had a conversation with this person and empathetically felt some of the feelings that this person felt during and after.

How to Read This Book
My advice is not to read this book in one go. Or if you do, come back to it and try the exercises in waves. Surfers know not to try and catch every wave. The same goes for this book. Be led by your inner compass to try the exercises found throughout this book. You'll know which ones are for you right now, and which ones to wait on. There's a lot of information in this book, so give yourself the opportunity to ride each wave in your own time. Coast the pages at your personal pace. Everyone's path is unique in this world.

A Companion
Keep this book around on the appropriate shelf or in an electronic folder so it will be waiting for you to come back to it whenever you are seeking more inspiration and guidance from it's pages. This is a companion book. It will keep you company on your journey.

Your Ongoing Commitment to Self-Care
Physical, sexual, and severe mental and emotional trauma affects the functioning of the brain. At first it also affects the ability of the body to rest soundly and sleep deeply. A tip for getting yourself to sleep peacefully while undergoing the depth of the work that you will read in this book is to listen to the delta brainwave video suggested in the endnotes section of this book. A great night's sleep allows your brain and body to integrate all of the lessons found within these pages.

When navigating trauma drama, particularly in the beginning, people often try to surpass one another's stories by saying things such as,

"I've been through a lot worse than that!" Or, *"That's nothing compared to what I've experienced!"* This book is not written with the spirit of comparing the size of our scars. This is not about "Your scar is bigger than mine." Or, "My scar is bigger than yours." After all, competition that results in the proclamation that any of us knows pain greater than another is fruitless. Comparison of whose pain is greater is *victim talk*.

By contrast, sharing our stories is how we get to know one another, trust, and bond. If and when this is the purpose behind our sharing we take a giant leap forward. With this intent, we benefit by taking a big picture view of our lives. We also create the opportunity to enrich and enliven the connections that we make along the way with the spirit to *rise* from the depths of our past trauma(s). Sharing our personal stories is indeed powerful.

In the United States people are becoming more trauma aware with the month of May appointed as *National Trauma Awareness* month and the day of June 27th being *National PTSD Awareness Day*. These are signs that it is becoming more widely accepted to open up and share your stories with your chosen community(ies).

PART ONE

Creating Understanding

☙

CHAPTER 1

What Is Trauma?

❧

WHAT IS TRAUMA? OR MORE IMPORTANTLY, how is it perceived and understood in today's culture?

A search of the word *trauma* on Google.com described it as a noun meaning:

1. A deeply distressing or disturbing experience.
2. A physical injury.

On the other hand, a visit to Merriam-Webster.com gives the meaning:

1. A very difficult or unpleasant experience that causes someone to have mental or emotional problems, usually for a long time.
2. A serious injury to a person's body.

The root of trauma in Greek is the verb *titrōskein*, which means "to wound."

The American Psychological Association website explains what happens when we experience trauma, describing it as "an emotional response to a terrible event like an accident, rape, or natural disaster. Immediately after the event, shock and denial are typical. Longer term reactions include unpredictable emotions, flashbacks, strained relationships, and even physical symptoms like headaches or nausea. While these feelings are normal, some people have difficulty moving on with their lives. Psychologists can help these individuals find constructive ways of managing their emotions."

In this book, *trauma* is described as any life event, whether it be physical, sexual, or mental in nature, that comes as a shock to your central nervous system and shakes your core beliefs about yourself and the world. Without a doubt, guidance and support are needed in order to move past the details of a traumatic life experience.

CHAPTER 2

What Is Trauma Drama?

❧

NOW THAT THE NATURE OF trauma is detailed, let us take a comparable look at the definition of the term *drama*. Google provides the definition as being:

1. A play for theater, radio, or television.
2. An exciting, emotional, or unexpected series of events or set of circumstances.

Whereas the Oxford Dictionary offers:

"To exaggerate the importance of a minor problem or incident."

Drama, which has an unspoken derogatory connotation across cultures, has several synonyms according to the same source, including "causing a scene, spectacle, crisis, disturbance, commotion, turmoil."

If trauma leads to emotional drama, how then is *trauma drama* defined? My definition is that it is the effect of carrying things like life events, situations, or people along with you even though they are no longer involved in your present life or physical circumstances. Additionally, trauma drama is the byproduct of excessively focusing more on other people than on yourself or on your life—to the extent that it produces a negative impact on you and your life.

It's no wonder that we like to create drama in our lives, considering that the root of the word *drama* in Ancient Greek is "to do, to take action." Most of us are desperate, either consciously or subconsciously, to effect change in our lives. When we see drama in our lives, more times than not it is the result of unconscious narratives in our minds that have not been sorted out, mostly because we, ourselves, are unaware that they even exist. It's important to learn how to realize the effects of our personal traumas on our lives so that we can graduate from being unconscious drama creators to being conscious satisfaction dwellers.

Are we making life more difficult than it needs to be for us? Can we open to the possibility of our lives being full of ease, so that our energy is freed to allow our lives to blossom in new and enjoyable ways? The realization made through universal life experience that life will *and does* throw all sorts of unpredictable circumstances our way can be particularly exhilarating, *and* monumentally terrifying all at once. Add a recent trauma to our experience and life's unpredictability can be downright horrifying. However, life's surprises, in and of themselves, can challenge us to new and previously inconceivable levels of happiness. When we approach the unexpected in a constructive way life's unpredictability is rewarding and the potential for drama is transformed from within.

On the other hand, if we do not find a way to extinguish, manage, and accept *and* honor the impact of our traumas accordingly, we will never be able to embrace life to its fullest and will more than likely continue to create unconscious dramas out of anything and nothing!

When I was researching the subject of emotional drama online, I happened to notice that each of the examples found regarding the usage and examples of the word itself referred to women who were being 'overly dramatic'. For example, UrbanDictionary.com and a contributing writer's, 'FreudianSlip' rather insensitively refers to trauma drama as:

The latest tale of woe from a Trauma Queen or Trauma Junkie. For example:

Mizzy's latest trauma drama was that her boyfriend hadn't called her in the last twenty minutes and must therefore be dumping her.

In my opinion, this definition trivializes trauma drama. Within this book, *trauma drama* is the term used to describe frequent and unnecessarily intense moments that interrupt your life and have their roots in a past trauma. Let's say that this fictitious character Mizzy had a dad that took off in the family Buick when she was a kid and was never seen again. The occasion of her boyfriend being out of touch longer than she is accustomed to therefore is an emotional trigger for her, reminding her of the invisible, yet deep and painful, wound that was caused by her father abandoning the family unit as a whole when she was a child.

Trauma is a dynamic state of being that each of us addresses within our lives. It is not to be mocked or minimized. Nor is it to be genderized as being attributed to being female or male. It is a real phenomenon and will at some point occur in everybody's life. It also is something that is workable, alterable, and, with thorough conscious evaluation, capable of being changed as a whole so that fortunately we can be liberated from yesterday if that is what we want. If we want to conquer our trauma drama, before we do anything else in an effort to heal we must cultivate compassion for ourselves by realizing what the stories of our lives are, what the *impact* of traumas within our lives are, and how we want to reroute our lives depending on our desired state of being.

This book presents the opportunity to show those who are aware of their struggle with trauma drama how to harness more self-control, to create a positive representation and perception of themselves, and to develop more appreciation for their lives in the biggest picture possible. To move beyond trauma drama is to find more ways to love yourself *no matter what may be going on in your immediate or distant surroundings.*

EXAMPLE OF TRAUMA DRAMA

Here is an example of trauma drama from my own life that may help you relate to what trauma drama is as well as to determine how it shows up for you.

Thinking that my power had been taken away by the man who was my rapist, and looking to "get that power back," I spent a few years of my life looking to be validated by men of great stature whom I chose to be my boyfriends, single men who ran global companies and were strong leaders in their communities and professional fields. I wanted to have my life given back to me by a "man in power" *because I believed it had been taken away by a man in power.*

As I grew up and into myself by developing *who I am,* I began to realize that I am no different from these men in my capacity to reign over my life with effectiveness and success.

ANOTHER EXAMPLE

In the household where I grew up there was much fighting among my siblings for the attention of our parents. My mother and father, the pillars of our family, were in high demand as one was constantly working and the other was ill in bed and in a state of rest. As it is with all people, some people get along with more ease than others because of their personality and dispositions. I adored my father and habitually would check in on him to see if he was okay, ask what he needed, and ask him to tell me stories of his great and long life before we were born. Perhaps I did this a little more than both of my sisters; it was said by many that my father scared them with his fierceness and impatience when he was around with the family. I didn't allow these traits to bother me and would often laugh at them when they were being displayed.

Growing up, I was taunted as being, "Daddy's Little Girl" and "Princess" because of the special bond between me and my father. For whatever reason these tensions were not resolved in my childhood. As a teenager and adult, I sensed through violent words and actions that my blood-related sisters were not happy with me. For many years, I forgave easily and would make it a point to spend my once-a-year vacation from my home in Vancouver, Canada, to be with my sisters in their respective towns and homes. Although the interactions were still disturbing for me, marked by unpleasant words and actions, for many years I gave my vacation days to them.

Finally, I realized that I was caught up in a cycle of trauma drama: a story of self-blame. For whatever reason, my subconscious self-interpreted my sisters' discontent in their adolescent and teenage years as being my fault. I had taken on too much responsibility for their interpretations of their childhoods. Whereas, it is known that my father loved all of his daughters the same. As a child, my father, in his sickness, told me that, "All I want is to be able to see my daughters grow up." In talks with me he verbally confirmed his love for me and my sisters, in moments such as these. This confirms that he did and, in spirit, still does love them very much.

It was only through my awareness of my internal narrative and noticing how I had created a cycle of drama that was causing me to stray from allowing myself a full life marked by deservingness, happiness, and mutual kindness in my relationships that I truly gained freedom from this particular trauma drama in the past.

The shifts and growth in my own life is how I know that these methods, principles, exercises, and tools are of assistance in the effective healing of trauma drama.

CHAPTER 3

Transforming Our Response to Trauma

❧

IN THIS BOOK, IN ADDITION to healing from our own traumas, we're also going to discuss, evaluate, and modify how we respond to other people's traumas. Here's an illustration of what NOT to do. If you feel it is best to skip this part of the chapter or book please feel free to continue on at the next bold heading found below.

When most people hear that a loved one has experienced a life-altering, totally-unpredicted, traumatic event, they almost immediately respond with, *"That's horrible!"* By responding this way, they are shutting off their minds and hearts to learning what the event *really means* to that loved one in an emotional and mental sense *and* life impact wise. The truth is, whether or not speakers like this have any ability to help a person manage the side effects of their trauma, in this moment they have forgotten to simply listen and *be present* without labeling the experience as being *one thing* or another. People who learn of a loved one's hardship are too often so appalled that "it" (whatever it is) has taken place that they sit in a stupor while the story of the incident is being told instead of cultivating presence with the survivor as attentive listeners.

However, when and if you are talking to a friend or family member who has experienced a trauma that involves a violation of personal boundaries, secondary harm can also be caused in direct proportion to how you respond to the information being shared with you. It's best to say, "I am here for you" or "What might I be able to do to help" rather than labeling the news with a doubly negative perception thereby reinforcing what is already evident in the situation, such as *"That is horrible..."*

Although the information in this book centers on your personal relationship with trauma, and its oftentimes resulting and unnecessary drama, it is worthwhile to consider how we view and respond to other people's traumas, as well as our own, partly so as not to haphazardly intensify the traumatization of the people we know and facilitate more unconscious drama in both their lives and ours.

As you have now read in the introduction of this book, I have had my own share of trauma and I assert that how I *digest* the experience and *live* out the unavoidable karma of these events has been by my active *choice*, as I assure you it is for you...how you digest and live out the karma of your traumas is your choice and only your choice.

The great news is that karma, in and of itself, is neither good nor bad. It is an openly interpretable force of the universe, *which is guided by how we perceive things.*

We often think that we know the facts of the situation when we hear about someone dying or being murdered, raped, or robbed. When we hear the news of a traumatic event, we may think about it for a flash of a second, but then, more times than not, we forget about it. We fail to think more deeply about the people behind the experience. What was that like *for them?* What difficulty did the trauma cause them or is still causing them *now?* Of course, we recognize that traumas are horrible occurrences. Some of us may even send out prayers or sympathy. But when we do, it's still often from a distanced, unempathetic place; we judge other people's traumas as something that *happened to* them and hope that something similar never happens to us.

Not the case. What happens to one of us happens to *ALL* of us. By observing the immediate reaction that we have upon hearing earth-shattering news, it's evident that we really cannot help realizing that the event has equally affected us. We deny this only because we feel scared by the news, possibly even shell shocked by its details.

For those of us who identify ourselves as survivors, we must remember that the process of mental, physical, emotional, and spiritual upheaval we've been through has changed us. Perhaps one of the greatest advantages we gain from accomplishing our own forward steps of healing is that we may respond differently when in connection with other victims in the future.

If we see a stranger on the street that looks hungry, we may give this individual a sandwich without hesitation. Goodness is such an integral part of our being on this earth that we don't ask *why* the person is hungry, sad, or despondent. We don't ask *why* the person isn't thriving. We don't ask what a hungry street person needs in order to buy a sandwich. We do not ask what such a person would change if he or she could change anything.

We give to hungry people what we can. From our hearts. From our hands. From our personal will to help. You see, as survivors of life's traumas and as observers of others experiencing trauma there is so much G(o)od in each of us when we only allow ourselves to act on our natural compassion.

We simply need to be more educated about the nature of trauma so that we can offer assistance to traumatized peoples as easily as we hand out sandwiches.

Not only do we need to be educated about what trauma is, but about the effects of trauma and the remedies for those effects of trauma. This blend of knowledge coupled with the spirit of human wisdom is crucial to helping survivors get the engines of their lives running.

How to Be of Help to a Loved One

A teacher of mine once said, "When you have a feeling and I identify with your feeling, it is *empathy*. Empathy is an internal process that we very much have command over—it is therefore not a passing feeling that may come or may go as it wishes. It is something that we cultivate out of love for the people both new and old in our lives.

This is what I have to say to extend these thoughts. What *doesn't* help with the healing of our loved ones' traumas or the drama that potentially will result is sympathizing *with the circumstances and events.* Saying obvious statements such as, "What a horrible event." does not help the survivor realize anything beyond what has already happened. Sympathizing with the actual physical events and circumstances energizes an individual's victim story and builds on the negative aspect of the past experience.

This does not serve the survivor.

Empathizing, which is identifying with the *feelings and emotions* of our loved ones, by contrast helps them be where they are in the *process* of their recovery *without* stirring up or stewing in the particulars of the events that they have experienced in the past.

Feelings and emotions by nature have a transient being so rather than being scared by the full range of what a survivor is feeling, support the rising and falling of each of the feelings and emotions as they come and go.

The *unspoken* feelings that you *sense* within a survivor naturally rise and fade.

The emotions that are *being expressed,* which you can see by their outward expression, rise and fade, too.

This is all healthy.

CHAPTER 4

How to Become a Novice of Your Own Experience

✺

YOU KNOW WHAT HAPPENED TO you on the outside when you underwent a trauma, but do you know what happened to you on the *inside* during and after you experienced this trauma? Equally as vital, do you know what happened to you *because of* that trauma?

Very often survivors of trauma can easily recount the details of what physically happened to them, but cannot go much further. This might be due to the fact that we live in a society where people don't talk much about what happens inside them. Although survivors of trauma feel angry and sad, and a whole range of other emotions, they also are likely to feel numb for a while because of the shock of the event. Because of this, they often have trouble sorting out their feelings. It's tempting for some survivors to deny the event and try to get on with their lives.

People around them are often in denial, too.

After experiencing a rape at age seventeen, all I knew was that I had experienced a physical event. That was really all I could tell anyone about it. I knew that my body was numb and sore and that I now suffered stomach upset on a regular basis, but for a long time I was unwilling to talk about or explore the sadness and rage within me. Because of sometimes feeling engulfed by my memories of the experience there was the sense of being locked into it. Because of the unmet and unexplored fear

I felt about what I had experienced all alone in that New York brown-stone I suppressed any curiosity to understand it.

Curiosity and the willingness to explore the response to trauma can give an ordinary person wings. It was when I began to observe without judgment how my trauma had impacted me that I took my first step onto the path of healing.

My question to you is this...

Do you know how your trauma has affected you?

We know when it happened. We know where and with whom. We might even know approximately how long the event lasted. We also likely have analyzed why it happened and with due reason: The little parts of us and the grandiose, soul-searching, larger-than-life parts of us are always trying to figure out why things happen in our lives. The danger is that we phrase the questions we ask as: "Why did this happen *to me?*"

To me, in particular, is the language of victimhood, a way of thinking and speaking that is to be avoided from now on because of how it keeps us anchored in a sense of victimization.

Hopefully, on this journey we choose the versions of why, what, who, when, and how that most liberate us and satisfy that part of us that wants to learn and grow past the limitations of our lives' most unexplainable and altering experiences. We want to shift from victims to survivors— and ultimately to become *thrivers*—with as much grace and dignity as possible.

Dignity comes from within.

We cannot always change how people view us and our life's experiences, but we definitely can change how we do.

How Have You Been Changed by Trauma?

Your trauma may be recent. Your trauma may have occurred long ago. No matter how long ago it occurred and no matter how much time and space lies between you, as you are today, and the experience, what changes do you see in yourself that are a result of the trauma?

What might you feel as I invite you to think about how your life has changed? I know what some people feel: anger, sadness, and disgust are common visitors to the moment. Whatever you are feeling is fine and healthy.

The fact is, examining painful events can be triggering, so at this moment I encourage you to take whatever action brings you ease. Both in mind and body. If thinking about these details is in any way upsetting. It's OK to move slowly through this book. Whenever you're ready, continue reading. Otherwise, I invite you to explore the answers to these questions with pen and paper.

What is it that you can see or sense that has changed in your life since the event of trauma?

Some changes are visible. Perhaps your smile isn't as bright as it was.

Some changes are sensed. Perhaps you don't light up over the simple things in life anymore, like the rare beauty of flowers and sunsets and luminescent moons, for the time being.

Some changes are behavioral or social. Perhaps you are avoiding certain activities now or reacting differently when people say or do things that you do not understand.

Maybe you want to light up and smile, but maybe you think that you cannot and question whether or not you'll ever be able to again. If so, rest assured, you aren't alone in this boat, and there is land in sight. As a collective whole, there is nobody anywhere in this world who can avoid being affected by one thing or another in this life. Everybody is impacted by life's experiences, some of them being trauma.

Before reading further, really take a moment to observe some of your changes.

Then carry on to the next section of this book.

EMBRACING THE TOTALITY OF YOUR EMOTIONS

Now that you've observed the changes that your experience of trauma has brought to your life, are you able or willing to be compassionate with yourself in this healing journey? Can you respect that you have been doing your best to survive your trauma?

When we look at our feelings and our behavior, it's really important to look at ourselves as we would look at a dear friend, with incredible compassion and unconditional regard.

With this in mind, I want you to know that I myself honor your feelings of sadness, anger, and confusion. It is OK and healthy to feel everything you feel here on these pages. Never apologize for having emotions. I also want you to know that I don't perceive you as broken or damaged. I don't pity you or imagine you in any way shape or form as being permanently bound to your circumstances.

It is my philosophy that when you tell someone that you feel bad for them it's the equivalent of telling them that they're bound to their circumstances, helpless and incomplete in their experience as they are. Doing this has the potential to diminish their life force and yours.

It's also okay to feel great AND fantastic, if that's what you feel. It's OK to feel sad one minute and happy the next. That's how emotions work! They are supposed to be fluid, ever-moving, and often without anticipation. Our society is so distanced from emotion that much of society fears the mere arising of the varying degrees of them.

If we continue to see emotions (whether joyful or angry) as being unacceptable, then we will push back against them and resist getting to know them. In this case, we become victims to our emotional states, rather than anticipators and masters, in the dark as to which emotion will come next. When we welcome each of our emotions as part of our being and an expression of our souls, then we empower ourselves to graduate to becoming masters of each state.

To educate means to 'bring out' and 'lead forth.' Also, to 'unfold' and 'draw out the powers of the mind'; this cannot be done without acquainting ourselves with each and every part of our being. If our mind, whether consciously or unconsciously, stifles the arising of an internally felt sense then we are consequently ignorant to one or vastly more components of ourselves. No good ever comes from ignorance.

No emotion is more acceptable than another. No matter what society does or doesn't think the reality is, each emotion—in a very real sense— is equally a part of our being. Pain is as real as joy. Joy is as real as pain. When we stop avoiding our emotions and the different mental states that arise as byproducts of our emotional selves, we come in contact with our individual truths. The more acquainted we become with our truth, the more comfortable we become with each part of ourselves. Our emotions in time become our long-lost allies: And no matter how much time has passed between visits with our friends, we must be prepared to welcome them. To connect with them. To love them for who and what they are.

EMOTIONAL NUMBNESS

Sometimes after trauma, when feelings and their resulting emotions are either intense or negative, we, as survivors, feel that it is unsafe to move into our emotional selves for fear of being continuously overwhelmed. A part of us often deems us incapable of handling the full breadth and range of emotion and feeling that accompanies our trauma. Both feelings and emotions can seem unsafe when they point to the reconnection of the moment when the original trauma had occurred. A feeling is the sensation we have internally, the sense, the emotion is the feeling expressed outwardly either when alone or in public.

Here is a writing and imagination exercise to practice when you're having an especially challenging time connecting to your feelings and therefore with your emotions.

Turn on your favorite TV show. As you watch the characters on the program living the individual moments of their lives, write down what you feel. If this is a challenge, for the time being then write down what you *imagine* they're feeling.

Then, write the sentences in the imaginative sense: "if I were _____ (name a character) and _____ (name an experience the TV character is having in as brief a manner as possible), I would personally be feeling _____ (make a guess).

In this next step, *think about* and then *write down* the three biggest life events that you're experiencing *right now* in *your* life that you are having a challenging time weighing in on how you feel about them.

Thirdly, write down this realization statement, "If I were watching my experience from afar, I'd be feeling _____."

Finally, to complete this whole exercise write down a first-person sentence: "I feel _____ (Place the feelings that you've identified in the previous step in the blank.) as I experience these major life events right now."

This is a great way to begin to both realize and connect with your *feeling* self.

INTENTIONAL RECONNECTION

To become a novice in our lives again means to reclaim the wonder and all of life's innate beauty. It is everywhere! Opening our eyes to the one within us is the first start to opening our heart to a new life. One time I overheard a stranger say something wise, "Let's make better mistakes tomorrow." I heartily concur with this idea. Making a mistake is far from the end of the world...at least not if we are leading healthy and fulfilling lives. In our lifetimes, we will start over again and again, a million and one times, if we're living life effectively.

In this book, I intend to show you that although trauma is shocking and painful, it also frees us in specific ways that make changing our lives into the happiest versions possible. As the result of a trauma, you are now blessed with the impetus to look deep within and are even being given an opportunity to change some of the causes and effects within your life.

If how I have described trauma drama in Chapter 2 resonates with you, and if you have identified with elements of it as being part of your life today, it is possible that you do not (yet) fully know what happened to you as a result of your trauma. This means how you were affected mentally, physically, emotionally, and spiritually. This is because of one reason alone: You have yet to fully give yourself the opportunity to explore it. That exploration needs to be undergone on four levels of your reality, as they are intertwined.

* The mental
* The emotional
* The physical
* The spiritual

For example, in the past, as a result of my life's traumas, I experienced physical discomforts. When I realized these were changes connected to the mental, emotional, and spiritual effects of my trauma, I understood more how to heal them. For example, after my rape occurred I had a perpetually sore left hip for approximately two years after the experience of kidnap and rape. If this type of soreness occurs today, I know how to soothe and extinguish the aching, discomfort, and limited range of motion that are involved with the side effects. I am able to sense any pangs coming on and I have a variety of solutions that I rely on to shift from soreness to ease of movement.

They include any or all of the following: a hot bath, one or two yoga stretches, self-massage, professional massage, reiki, a long walk and craniosacral therapy.

It was my willingness to explore post-traumatic changes that enabled me to engage with neglected, almost forgotten parts of myself. I became empowered as a result of driving my focus inward. As a result, I was even given the opportunity to be closer to myself, the one person I had tried so hard to avoid after the most significant traumas of my life. In this life we can entertain fear to our detriment or we can allow the spirit of curiosity, born from--but not always recognized as--love, to push its way into every part of our existence.

Are you familiar with that saying, "Do what is easy and your life will be hard; do what is hard and your life will be easy?" Well, it just so happens that God, Source, the Creator of All, is a big proponent of this particular theory. And I mean BIG. If you put yourself out there every day the heavens will sparkle in your honor. If not right away then before too long, sure enough you will reap the benefits of living a brave and curious life sourced from love.

I invite you to go within your extra-ordinary self as you continue to read these chapters.

A Deeper Exploration of The Four Components of Self

As I continued to take time to explore in search of what was going on inside my hip, I asked: What feelings do I have when I sense the feeling state of my left hip?

The answer was "unsafe and, in general, insecure." I also felt "out of balance."

Then I asked: What ideas, relationships, or activities have I over-invested in that have created a block against feeling safe, secure and balanced? (Now that I knew the emotional aspect of the hip situation, I wanted to know the mental aspect.)

As my mind reflected on this question, I found that as a child I had invested too much energy in everyone else's needs, putting them ahead of my own—a behavior that I saw modelled by my mother who was financially responsible for three daughters plus endless medical bills for my father. I was also commended by my mother for putting everyone else ahead of me since that is what she also had done to extreme levels. Thankfully, in later years, she would grow out of this behavior and rearrange her priorities to include her own inner well-being, too.

As I recognized the above, I decided that I would begin an inward journey to rediscover my personal needs. Knowing and deciding that I was *worthy* enough to go on this adventure was my spiritual growth, and this realization met the necessary spiritual component of the self-inquiry process.

In order to alter the behavior of putting other people before me, I decided that I would learn how to engage in healthy communication. A cornerstone of healthy communication is identifying what our individual needs are and, in this example, being courageous and daring enough to communicate them.

The effects?

My family thought me selfish for doing so.

I stopped being plagued by sore hip syndrome.

Thankfully, I had already crossed over the stepping stone in my life to realize that I could not control how other people think or feel about living out the truth of my heart, body, and soul. So, I was freed from needing to take any further action beyond letting my immediate family know that I loved them and wished them to live happy and fulfilled lives. From that moment forward, I became incredibly free to live my *own* life.

. . . Defining Your Own Reality. . .

Did you know that you can feel however you want to feel? You can! Here's how.

First, choose precisely what you want to feel.

Then, allow yourself to cultivate a rich and deep experience of wanting this emotional state of being.

Then, invite the feeling into your gut. Decide that this can and will be your experience.

In order for something to become our genuine experience, we must set ourselves up for it to be so. We must meet the experience halfway. To meet your desired emotional state halfway, think about and feel into your close relationships, either business or personal: What might you want to adjust in your actions to meet the experience halfway?

It is true that we cannot change how other people act, think, or speak. We can only change ourselves. The great news is that there are millions of people in the world who will align with our newly specified and chosen actions and desires, even if some of the people in our lives will not.

Regardless of whether or not your family or your present friends and colleagues are willing to meet your needs, or have the ability to meet them, I hope that you are motivated to cultivate relationships with people who can and want to meet them. *New* **circumstances, involving new levels of acceptance and belonging, will occur because of your willingness to design life anew.**

If you do not know what you are capable of yet, don't worry. That's normal. Let me assure you that you are beyond the norm *because* you have decided to explore and discover the effects of your traumatic experience on your world *today*.

Own that distinction: *You are capable.*

The most important analysis to make at this juncture is what healthy changes you can make in your life by learning *how* you were impacted by the trauma. Learning how you were affected is a show stopper for drama! Drama cannot live in your shoes...if you decide to walk the path of discovery.

A Note About the Breath

As it flows, the breath helps to connect us to the source of all of life. Like the days and moments of our lives, the breath is always naturally shifting and moving on with or without us. It is the mind that sits with confliction that has the potential to interfere with our breath. So, how may we surrender to the moments of our lives and continue to flow just as our breath does? The answer is *through* our breath. We surrender by being honest with ourselves and accepting of how we are feeling in every moment.

Like so many others on the path of inner realization, I am convinced that every living being on our planet is shaped by its environment and experiences. We humans are shaped more than other creatures by the thoughts that we choose. We have heard time and time again that we are *not* our experiences but rather *what we make* of our experiences. This reminds me of the fact that when angered or upset we are not truly mad at others; we are mad *at their behaviors.* This takes the energy off of the intensity of the moment and the emotional hurt and places significance on *behaviors* that are not working for us and perhaps are not working for the other person, either.

Though the first stage of both healing and connecting to our breath is the acceptance of our experiences, I believe we also need to remind ourselves that we can grow from them by dressing ourselves with a new layer of experience. This new layer is one of decided knowing that there is something you have yet to discover about the full potential of who you are. The imprint of past experience can be removed from being the dominating fact of our consciousness by *fully* having the felt experiences we are having today.

Our breath is a key that opens doorways within us with each inhalation. On each exhalation, it becomes a vehicle that allows us to let go of an old layer of felt experience and predominating thought consciousness. As a yoga guide, I like to remind myself and others: *The breath, whether it is an inhalation or an exhalation, is most rewarding when it precedes new thoughts and new actions.*

The experience of the breath occurring in sync with or just before new felt experience and cognitive realization offers the individual an experience *of the moment.* This experience is of mind and body connecting together. In yoga postures this is true both for leading into a pose and for exiting from a pose. *Breath comes first . . . and initiates both movements.* The inner warrior's path is to realize the next movement before thoughtfully carrying it forward into the world.

As we mindfully breathe during the moments of our lives, we gain more inner power and simultaneously become more connected to the Source of all that is. As Thich Nhat Hahn has said, *"To be alive is to know God; to know God is to be alive."* Whether you relate to Goddess(es), Source, God, Buddha, Atma, or another name for the Divine, this awareness of the benefit of embodying breath is essential for bringing us closer to the experience of all that is.

Let us practice this mantra—or repeated thought—together as we breathe.

"I trust the movement and changes of life to bring excellent experiences, people, things, beings, and places to me . . ."

Breath is the direct experience of our individual spirit as it moves through us. Are we fully embracing life? Are we allowing breath to move through us? Are we claiming our experience in this moment? Are we owning the *trust* that life is exactly what we need for it to be? That any changes we want to make we are fully capable of making by sheer choice? That if change cannot happen by the making of one choice, do we trust that through making several smaller choices or decisions we *can* make the impact we desire?

CHAPTER 5

Drama is a Fact of Life,
Like it or Not!

༄

PASSION IS AN INTEGRAL PART of being human. The real question is: Are we using that fire energy for self-growth and the cause of becoming a happier, lighter, and more fully self-expressed human being or not? Human emotions are a fact of life. Are we using ours to become more effective in the management of our lives? Or are they out of control?

Here is an example that allows us to explore the role of emotions in transformation, which shows how our emotions can serve as catalysts for the most powerful kind of change there is: *change within.*

A woman and a man are in a committed, romantic relationship. The man is in charge of managing a popular restaurant in a big city. In fact, it is the same place they met when he was enjoying the ambiance of the establishment on his day off. During a full year of togetherness, he has asked his significant other not to come there again because it is where he works. But she wants to go for two reasons: first, because it reminds her of the day they met; second, because it happens to be a wonderful, well-known restaurant with such great food and atmosphere that all the other restaurants in the neighbourhood pale in comparison to it.

The couple's relationship is now waning and the woman wants out. She's tired of limiting her life to what her boyfriend recommends that she do or not do. While respecting his wishes about not hanging out with her while he's working, she wants to live freely. As a remedy for her sense of restriction and to break out of the mold that her boyfriend has set for her, she decides she'll begin to live her life as she pleases, including going to the places that she wants to go. When Thursday night rolls around, she goes to the popular restaurant her boyfriend manages with a close girlfriend of hers to have dinner. In order to respect her partner's desire for space, she sits as far as humanly possible away from the bar. She focuses entirely on having a great time with her friend and sits in such a way that she's not even looking in her boyfriend's direction. The next day, the man informs the woman that he never wants to speak to her again.

The upset between the couple leads both to develop greater inner strength and self-realization. The woman, once she is no longer subordinating her desires to the man's when it comes to making decisions, feels stronger and more connected to herself. Once the relationship is over, the man has realizations about himself, too, as a direct result of being upset with the woman. He learns the difference between making a demand with an ultimatum and and making a request.

In an optimal situation, both of these individuals would be living life in alignment with their individual and highest beliefs. This means that she would be more aware of her freedoms and of her self-worth and he would have greater awareness around his ability to be gentle in his communications, placing more emphasis on sharing what is truly bothering him and why.

Drama in the form of conflict and passion is unavoidable in our lives. Even well-intentioned people will find themselves in conflicts. As emotional beings and as individuals with different needs and desires, there will always occasionally be moments of conflict and negotiation in our lives. Let me be clear that I am *not* saying that drama *is* trauma. Or even, for that matter, that trauma is drama. Trauma drama is *unnecessary* drama that follows a trauma when it has not been processed fully. Trauma drama is a separate category of experience, something disconnected from the normal or typical associations we have with trauma or drama as individual forces.

UNNECESSARY DRAMA

Let's look at unnecessary drama. Unnecessary drama is drama in which the focus put on the conflict or on expressing a certain type of passion is life compromising. Philanderers, thieves, and murderers are often driven by their passions. But in being unethical by breaking agreements, stealing, and killing they cause pain and drama as they pursue their objectives. This type of drama is obviously life-compromising.

As we well know, all passion is not life-compromising. Passion that motivates constructive actions can be rewarding, and often life sustaining. Furthermore, if we are fighting for justice and standing up for our beliefs, or defending ourselves, something, or someone else that requires our support, then the passion—and the drama that may unfold as a byproduct—is very likely necessary.

Trauma and drama will be facts of life until 100 percent of the population is enlightened enough both not to *knowingly* cause another hurt as well as to be able to avoid *unknowingly* causing hurt. We cannot absolutely guarantee how others will interpret our actions and our thoughts; therefore drama may exist within our environment even when we do not understand the cause of it. It's important to note that we needn't make ourselves small by adding to drama that we do not initiate. Society often inadvertently implies that responding to people's dramas is the socially acceptable form of partaking in the moment.

Having drama within us is completely normal and human. We do have the choice, however, as to if we will bring other people into the drama within our minds, that our mind makes up, or to find a way to sort through and digest the natural drama that exists within our human predicament that involves us and us alone. This goes back to the methods listed earlier, such as writing things out before they get too out of hand. Or, in the case of fiery passion or anger, signing up for a kickboxing or acting class, where the acting or reflecting on and harnessing of emotions is necessary to succeed thus creating a sense of a positive outcome.

Really and truly, it is we, as people, who decide what the nature of a drama will be.

Imagine for a moment that the woman who dated the manager of the bar had created unnecessary drama in response to being kept at arm's length by her boyfriend. Let's say she had decided that she'd get back at him for not loving her the way she wanted to be loved. She might decide to take a guy who has asked her out to her former boyfriend's restaurant and then sit as close to the bar as humanly possible so they could be seen by the ex-boyfriend plus all his friends. Can you see the difference in those actions from the ones I initially described? Can you also see that this second approach is devoid of opportunities for self-growth however it does bring about a cheap thrill?

Causing her former boyfriend discomfort or pain might have been her goal if she had pursued such a course, but it wouldn't have made them any better suited for one another anytime in the future. The momentary satisfaction would be the *best* thing drama could get her in this situation. In fact, if she makes this choice, even if the bar manager former boyfriend were to profess his undying love and need to be with her after seeing her with another man, the profession would be made from a place of insecurity and jealousy. That is not self-realized love. She would have manipulated him, pushing him to compete for her attention in response to an outside circumstance, rather than deciding to reconnect based on the love he feels for her as is.

This kind of life-compromising drama is unnecessary. It is the essence of trauma drama. When we create drama in our lives that has the intent of controlling other people's behavior because we're feeling emotionally triggered, it's important to stop and ask a fundamental question: *Am I reacting to the inevitable drama in my life in a way that is life constructive, or am I creating more drama than is needed now perhaps as a result of past traumas that I've experienced in my life?*

For the sake of this book, let's imagine that what drove the young woman in this story to enter into a relationship with a man who shuts her out and neglects her was that it was similar to the way she was brought up. The reason she has willingly tolerated his refusal to communicate with her if it is not on his own terms is that for many of her years as a young child she was often ignored. She grew up in an old-fashioned household where kids were supposed to be seen *and not heard.* Her parents were rarely home, and when they were, they were fending off depression, absorbed in their troubles, and more often than not inviting their kids to participate in their own activities rather than joining into the kids' preplanned activities. The parents were not bad people. They simply did the best that they could with the limited inner resources they possessed at the time due to not realizing their own trauma drama.

There was neglect, yet the understory that the woman developed as a girl was the belief that she was loved regardless of the neglect. As an adult, she told herself that this way of interacting with the core people in her life must be okay. Due to this particular belief and sense of how relationships are conducted, she drew partners to her who were similarly neglectful, and maintained the belief that despite of this she was truly loved by these men. Her boyfriends expressed deep care for her in the moments when they were present over the years. But in order to ultimately experience a well-rounded, well-adjusted love relationship she needed to break free of this pattern of relationship. The pattern itself often would ignite the emotions associated with the trauma of neglect from her childhood caretakers. This meant that each time her boyfriend ignored her for days or inhibited her from dining at the restaurant where he worked, her early-life trauma was re-experienced.

That is trauma drama.

By no means was this boyfriend a *bad* person. However, his method of connection was not well-suited to the needs of the woman's heart. He ultimately would find himself better served by being in relationship with a new girlfriend who didn't have similar childhood experiences as the woman in our story. He needed to be with someone who viewed his absence as a simple annoyance and not a heart-based problem.

CHAPTER 6

Top Seven Causes of Trauma Drama

✿

IN THIS CHAPTER, WE'LL EXPLORE seven of the top causes of trauma drama.

* Lacking awareness of triggers
* Language intended to harm
* Putting the onus on another
* Self-victimization that leads to loss of self
* Denial of facts
* Focusing on other people's agendas more than yours
* Projecting your reality on another

LACKING AWARENESS OF TRIGGERS

Here's an example of having a trigger in your blind spot: Let's say that someone has an excessive need to know that she's appreciated—more so than most of us. This need stems from her childhood, because she was never told that she was "good enough." Now, as an adult, she seeks appreciation from people everywhere she goes; getting validation from feeling well-regarded is like having a Band-Aid put on the childhood wound. She gives to people to prove to them that she is enough by their definition; however, she doesn't really feel fulfilled by this behavior because no one ever seems grateful enough for what she does.

One day, the woman explodes after giving a present to a friend who doesn't say thank you for the gift. This explosion ruins the friendship and leaves both the woman and her friend scratching their heads afterward and wondering what happened. Sure, the friend's manners could have been better, but the degree of pain that the lapse in manners caused the gift giver was disproportionate.

The trigger for the woman in this scenario was feeling unappreciated. She lacked awareness of her sensitivity, which came from the traumatic experience of being told she was not good enough by the people who were caring for her in her earliest years. That blind spot led to an explosion of emotion when she was triggered. She hadn't realized she was trying to compensate for the past by seeking constant approval by the people in her today.

Thankfully, being unaware of our triggers is a temporary issue. The remedy for being haphazardly triggered to the demise of our relationships is exploring the *abyss* of otherwise unrecognized pain within us *before* we spin out of control. After that, the subconscious is a powerful element of our psyche that can be reprogrammed with new beliefs and focuses to move forward.

Language Intended to Harm

There are remarks and statements that just flat out hurt. Once you get to know someone well you can pretty much guess what kinds of remarks bother them most. You can figure out what will take their breath away or cause damage. There are subconscious misperceptions as to why saying hurtful things will be of help in any given situation. We get the sense that we will be given freedom from the situation and from the pain that we are feeling in that moment, for whatever reason, and thus, *bang*, the words are spoken to impress whatever it is that you are trying to impress upon the other person.

Evil words can be spoken at times because we have the sense that we will convince the person who we are in disruption with to *back off* or *leave us alone*. They can be said at times to prove that we are *"right,"* or that we *"know better"* than the assailant with whom we are rough and tumbling energetically and verbally. Sometimes they can be said in an ill-attempt to gain control over the situation.

Let's say two teenagers, Amanda and John, get into a fight. Amanda says, "It's your fault that we can't go to the concert tonight because *you* didn't ask *me* before you lent *our* car out to *your* best friend!"

When this happens, John has two solution-focused choices to make. The first is to explain profusely and in great detail why he lent the car. The other is simply to say, *"I apologize. I'm doing my best. I made the best decision I knew to make in that moment."*

If we apologize with sensitivity and care versus with ambivalence and haste and if we are doing our part of connecting in a genuine fashion then from there it is the other individual's choice as to whether or not to accept you and your disposition. If they are meant to be in your life, most people will 100 percent leap at the opportunity to accept, let go and reconnect.

If you are reading this book, I know that you are a human being of great love and care. And, people of this nature, more times than not, attract people into their lives with similar predispositions. Having a sense of deserving for being treated in a kind way is equally as important when co-creating amendable situations.

The more we consciously *choose* to use words that open up roads of connection with other people and within ourselves, the more likely it is that we'll lead ourselves to experience fulfilling, profoundly-successful and blissful lives.

PUTTING THE ONUS ON ANOTHER

Without knowing it, when we use language that puts the onus on someone else we are often doing so to save ourselves from being alone with our pain. Whether we are doing it consciously or unconsciously, it's an invitation to bring a guest into our experience of pain.

Underlying every reality, there really are only two universal states of being: love or fear. Pain is a form of fear. We all are likely to experience fear periodically as long as we are on this planet. You may therefore see that the desire to peg responsibility on someone else's shoulders is an ill-attempt to be free of pain and fear itself.

In a moment of desiring reprieve from the existing in pain alone, might you knock on someone else's door and ask if they want to join you?

Is the desire to include others right or wrong, good or bad? Or, neither?

Think of someone who has made an irreversibly life-affecting mistake who is in so much pain and despair that they call the first person they can think may join them in the level of despair being felt. *Suppose that's you.* You are the person they are going to. Suppose they, at the root of their action, are experiencing fear and pain and despair, and yet they call you and scream in your face, claiming that you have done something terribly wrong.

Are you triggered? You bet.

But. . .

They are doing their best, no?

Now, what if this hypothetical screamer and blamer was you.

That can't be too hard to believe, yes?

After all, if you haven't done it today, you've done it in the past (unless you were born an enlightened apostle or Zen monk).

Even our best is not enough to compel ourselves forward sometimes; nor is it enough for those around us. Unfortunately, if our best comes from an unconscious, unevolved place, even our best is the cause of dysfunctional communication and disconnect.

What do we do in order to not place the onus of our pain on others? Well, that's a 'different-strokes-for-different-folks' kind of a situation. If you are the one placing the onus, then next time you go to do so, take a moment and ask yourself, *"Am I coming from pain? Am I looking for someone to join me in the pain? What's the best invitation that I can put forward?"*

Fortunately, a genuine apology, offered from a place of vulnerable self-expression, remedies miscalculated attempts at forming connection with others.

The Apology Mantra for Unforgiveness

"You know, God, I've apologized as much as I can without losing myself in this situation or person. I have my own soul song to dance. I allow you to continue to work in my life. I trust the process of living and loving now."

SELF-VICTIMIZATION

Self-victimization is a heady and deep undertaking to pull apart, but we'll go ahead and jump in together! Self-victimization is a rare phenomenon that eventually leads to loss of the self. An epic version of this is someone who has been through a life loss, such as a breakup, that's been coming for a long, long time and yet acts as if he or she CAN'T BELIEVE it's gone down when the time comes. (You can see how this also stems from a denial of the facts, which we'll talk about in the next section of this chapter.) Let's say this person focuses all day long on the woman who he's lost and why he's lost her. Because he's victimizing himself in this way, he loses himself, and his day, in seemingly unstoppable thoughts of the now-absent person.

Here's another example. Let's say that you lost your job. To think tirelessly about this *one* job leads to a loss of self AND all of the moments that may have been, had your mind not obsessed on the absence of that *one* career stepping stone.

When you think, for any length of time, about someone who is no longer in your life, or something that you are actually not doing, then that moment is being lost to other possible experiences. It is self-victimization because you are the only person who's losing anything. You are sending your energy away from yourself and whatever else makes up your life at this time and station of your life.

If you don't focus, then the train of life will leave the station without you. Life never waits. It asks us to show up, be present, and sit in the fires of self-transformation every day of our lives. If we do not have at least one epiphany each day, then we're as good as dead.

When it comes to self-victimization, and the chosen direction of our energy, whether it is a conscious or an unconscious decision, the time when the loss of a relationship is our present reality can be particularly challenging.

Here's why . . .

Thinking poorly of someone you are upset with is human nature. Notice I do NOT say that it is superhuman nature because we DO have the potential of elevating ourselves to the superhuman level, too! However, wishing someone would leave the face of the planet 100 percent lowers your energy level no matter how you look at it. It is the attaching of our 'victim story' to challenging emotions as they arise that permits negative thinking to prosper. Self-victimization is ALWAYS present in negative thinking.

So, when you are feeling victimized (a great indicator is when you are going on and on about one thing a*nd one thing only* that has to do with *other* people's actions) grab a hold of that emotion before it spins out of control and elevate yourself above that SHIT!

What is meant by that?!

Well, in our society, anger is looked down upon *a lot.* Only there is absolutely nothing wrong with anger itself. There can be something hurtful and unproductive about some of the ways that we express our anger. However, anger, in and of itself, is a potentially prosperity-creating feeling AND emotion. The trick is to know when you are *feeling* angry so that you can *emote* your anger in a way that satisfies the need to express it.

It is without a doubt that we all need to express our anger.

Let us then find healthy ways to do it!

One thing that I do is place a pair of Everlast boxing gloves in my office. My everyday aim is to walk to the punching bag (if I am traveling I walk over to the pillows on the guest bed) and start punching the bag nonstop for 1–2 minutes. That's all.

BAM! *An ounce of prevention equals a pound of cure!*

PRO: No one is hurt.

PRO: I do not regret feeling angry later.

PRO: I have exerted my muscles in a way that is both satisfying and healthy.

There are no CONS.

Sometimes, even when I am not feeling any anger I call on something in my life that I have yet to perhaps allow myself to feel fully and for those 60-90 seconds I pound away at the bag.

When we don't express or acknowledge our anger, whether it's over the injustices within our lives, troubles in the lives of our loved ones or strained relations in a community on the other side of the earth that we just watched a two-hour-long heart wrenching documentary about, it has the potential to become a *deep* sadness that gets locked inside of us. *Sadness becomes depression unless we use anger to liberate us from the dark hole of injustice.*

Now, boxing gloves and a punching bag may not be your cup of tea. If that's the case, then creating a focal point outside of your source of anger in which to pour the anger into is advantageous and *healthy*. Instead of yelling at the person you are upset with, you join a book club where everyone is pissed off about the wretched subject matter that you are enduring as a group. Or you join a hiking group and pound the dirt with your sneakers as you climb the hills or mountains nearby. Or, you healthily participate in a community theatre near you—if there isn't one *then start one.* MeetUp.Com or something of the nature in your time zone is next to free and an amazing source with which to create community literally out of thin air from your desktop computer.

Whatever you do, consciously choose activities so that they can be conduits in and of themselves for you to express the whole range of feelings that you're humanly experiencing.

Do not look to a fallen relationship to be your fix for your need to express all that you are going through. No one has enough time or energy to be your one point of contact for a particular issue in your life, even if it regards them. Remember that *everyone* is going through his or her own challenges emotionally, mentally, and spiritually, and we all have different ways of expressing our internal experiences.

Let's instead become superhuman and *choose* the way that we will relinquish the chains of unexpressed emotion.

Preparation is key...

I invite you *not* to victimize yourself by the belief that a particular person "does not want to be there for you" or "hates you" or "doesn't care about you" or "is trying to sabotage or ruin your life." It is sometimes impossible to be there for another when we ourselves are going through something challenging and it takes everyone different lengths of time to digest experiences—*especially conflicts.*

The best people to understand what you're going through are people who are going through what you are going through. Support groups are revolutionary in this sense.

Consider the following idea. Embracing any feeling that lies within the range of human experience is the way to empower yourself *and* leads to the healthiest expression of the feelings! Disempowered, ignored, and neglected feelings lead us to become disempowered, ignored, and neglected people who have little power over themselves or their experience.

One thing is absolutely certain: Life is too precious to give it up to one person or one set of circumstances just because you think the feelings associated are too much or hold power over you.

These people and feelings are your teachers. Look at them as such.

Get your boxing gloves on! You are the most powerful teacher in your *own* life!

Start to take actions to love yourself, love your feelings, and love your thoughts... Never give anyone else dominion over you, instead give the *best* parts of you to **YOURSELF**. They are *YOURS* to have, to love, and to embrace!

Honor your inner self every day.

Denial of Facts

After my kidnapping and rape as a seventeen-year-old in New York City, I actually told myself that the experience didn't happen. For approximately two years I denied it by simply walking away from it and not talking to anyone else about it. It was as if I was ten years old, again, walking the track with my classmate Brittany and upon hearing the word for the first time detached completely from its possibility.

"Do you know what rape is?" Brittany had asked me.

"Rake?" I puzzled, "You mean, when someone like 'rakes leaves'?"

"No. I mean when someone has sex with you even though you don't want it."

I couldn't fathom the new idea on that day, or seven years later when I was in New York.

It was because I didn't have any reference for the experience that it was altogether too overwhelming. I made a conscious choice, out of great, great fear to say to myself that it didn't take place. It was such a despicable occurrence that I wanted it never to have happened. Lying to myself and denying my trauma was the beginning of great illness in my body, mind, and spirit, a source of incredible drama.

If I couldn't be honest to myself then who else would I be able to trust enough to be honest with outside of myself? The answer was no one.

The problem with the approach of denial is that if we try and push feelings and thoughts away, the way I did with my post-trauma, they come back. If we try and ignore them or resist them, then they rule us and create drama in our lives...*instead of us ruling them.*

A Quick Lesson in Language: *Stop Denying YOUR Power!*

All phrases that include, "You 'made' me" or "You 'make' me!"

For example, "You *made* me fail." or "You *make* me angry." are catalysts for drama!

The following type of sentence puts power *outside of you* and gives it to another person or some imaginary "it."

"When someone yells, it scares me and *makes me* uncomfortable."

By contrast, this sentence creates a focus on *your* experience which is where *you are the one capable* of making changes. "When someone yells, I feel scared and I feel very uncomfortable."

Now, having made this observation, the ball is in your court to make changes. It empowers you because it acknowledges that you are the center of your personal story and the story is no longer projected onto someone else or something else.

OVERCOMING DENIAL: STOP LYING TO YOURSELF AND/OR OTHERS

Tell your truth. Hiding from our truths makes us small and weak, and therefore prey to repeating the same day over and over again.

Step out.

Tell the truth.

No truth is ugly. However, our response to it can be. It is crucial to realize that hiding is *not* an option in the facing and meeting of the extensive body of our dreams.

Denial is tricky. If you're "good" at suppressing information you don't want to know and feelings you don't want to feel, you might not know you're in denial. Nevertheless, it's possible to figure out whether you're in denial even if you're skillful at camouflaging your pain. The way is to use your body as your tool.

BEGIN

Suppose you're wondering what your true feelings are about a particular situation, event or person in your life. Focus on a word that you are *thinking* describes a feeling you have about the person/situation/event you have chosen for the time being. If you notice that you are having a cerebral experience of this feeling in the region of your head, neck, and shoulders, you may be in denial about how you are really feeling about it. If there is tension and sensation in this region, it usually means that you are not feeling the whole feeling (for example: anger or sorrow), but instead only tapping into the disconnected "head of the situation" versus tapping into "the heart of the situation". This means that you are having an isolated experience of a feeling because *for whatever reason* being connected to your feelings in their entirety has been perceived as dangerous in the past.

We are not actually feeling the whole experience of a challenging state unless we can invite it into the *whole body*. That's the rubric for ensuring authenticity *and thus embodying the fullness of each of our experiences.*

If you notice yourself getting caught up in the story of a feeling and having a heady experience versus the full experience, then focus on your breath. Invite your inhalations to expand into all parts of your chest cavity, stomach, intestines, all your organs and limbs. Invite the breath in again and again until you gradually become aware of your body's sensations as a whole experience and not a fragmented one.

After taking at least seven whole-body breaths, choose an anchoring statement. This is an affirmation whose purpose is to root you in the calm experience that you've just created for yourself by taking those deep whole-body breaths. The sentence will be unique to you so there is no wrong or right one.

If you like, you may also use this one to begin: *I recognize and honor myself as a divine being put on this earth to experience myself in both my fullness and greatness!*

Anchoring sentences must be phrased in the positive, so avoid sentences that sound like, "I do *not* feel _____" or "I *no longer* feel _____." Rather, say exactly what *does* invite calm and peace, and inspires you with the motivation to change in the proportion and ways you desire.

If you identify yourself as "someone who is just not good with words" and do not think you can do something like crafting an anchoring sentence, please keep trying. If you want help learning how to set your intention through words, you may set up a one-on-one consultation with me. *Visit DiscoverYourResilience.com and AdventuresInInk.com*

Focusing on Other People's Agendas More Than Yours.

Agenda simply means a list, plan, outline, or the like, of things to be done, matters to be acted or voted upon. To not be aware of your own agenda, aka plans in life, is to be self-effacing and certainly gearing yourself up for trauma drama rooted in the area of resentment that causes great conflict along the way. Definitions often refer to agenda in connection with work duties, however we all have plans for our lives outside of work, I hope. We are all aware that investing in our personal lives is equally crucial to do as it is to invest in our work lives.

The moment where the word *agenda* takes on an antagonistic spin is when people have plans that they are not telling other people around them although they are relying on that person or people to supply the needs of their agendas.

Let's consider that you as an adult are being forthright with communicating your plans with the people in your life with whom you have the closest connections with and whom you share a healthy interdependence with. Let's imagine that you are communicating what your plans are for the day, month, and year with these people or person. That is healthy agenda making and execution. However, if you are not talking to people who you have a deep bond with about your larger picture visions then that can be incredibly misleading and create issues down the road.

How much have you thought about your own life's agenda? It is crucial to balance Your agenda with the agendas of your loved ones to ensure against subjecting yourself to the whims and plans of someone else, and possibly in disproportionate levels. Suppose you think this person is the *cat's meow* and you can't imagine living without them so you surrender your part in constructing the daily, weekly, monthly *and* annual calendar. You say, "Whatever makes you happy." to nearly everything while deep down you are boiling at the fact that you have relinquished choice in these matters.

Well, do you care?

Do you care that you are missing out on the opportunity to collaborate and join energies, and instead are giving all your energies away to someone who you believe is more fit and capable of carrying out the daily orders?

If you want to be brimming with joy and satisfaction at living a whole life then I highly suggest getting courageous and speaking out your truth to those who you care about. No one else can, but you.

Dating back as far s the 17th century, 'agenda' has simply and dearly meant, 'things to be done.' If this section applies to you, I suggest that you get out a pen and paper and write down exactly what it is that you see as a necessity for your own life so that when the time comes to exit this world you have the sense that you have stood tall, firm, purposeful *and* strong in your knowing that you have a place in this world all on your own.

PROJECTING YOUR REALITY ONTO ANOTHER

Projecting your own reality onto another is equally as damaging if not more than giving unsolicited advice.

We as people each have a *feeling* about a moment and our *sense* or intuition about a moment. Although these two assemble what we individually experience as truth, in our perception, and as truth in our personal lens, everyone else we cross on our way to school, work, play is also experiencing their own unique, individual and authentic *feeling* of the moment and thus overall *sense* of the moment. That's why we have court judges and lawyers because the truth must be arrived at through a variety of blended facts, from a variety of people's perspectives and individual interpretations of multiple events.

Think back to a time when you had a completely different experience than someone else did although the experience's two main characters were both you and that person and that's it. No one else. Two different people, two totally different lens. These two people wind up confused and likely frustrated because one person's feelings about a situation and their recounting of its details pale in comparison to the other person's recollection of it. This is a classic experience that makes up many of our lives at one point in time or another.

The challenge here is when you are denying that the other person's experience holds any weight, or "that it didn't happen at all." Now, depending on how much the other person involved is confusing the situation, the outcome can either be comical or downright exhausting. If you're trying to prove that your reality, way of seeing, experiencing, feeling and sensing were the only true variables, and discounting the other person's then you are going to be downright exhausted and disenchanted with finding a solution. On the other hand, whether or not amends are a possibility or not, if you are compassionate by acknowledging the other person's variables then you are going to discover freedom in the situation. Your mind will open. The headache will subside. The heart will soften.

Not everyone is meant to be best friends. However, cultivating the sense that there is always more than one reality and *honoring* that there is by not projecting the variables of your own reality: *your feelings, your sense, your perception, your past, your bias* onto everyone else is a key to your personal happiness and the fuel to continuing to pursue your own dreams because you are not weighted by the "need" for everyone else to see life as you see it.

There is nothing attractive about an overly-righteous person. Therefore, do not either outrightly say or imply that other people's realities "do not exist".

When we argue with someone about what did or did not happen first ask the person if they're willing to exchange the following shared details with you:

What is your sense of the experience that is upsetting you?

What are your feelings? (Remember to mark feelings as *words such as "embarrassed"*, not as perceptions like "I feel you're trying to embarrass me." That is not a feeling--that is your filter of the situation.)

Next,

Is it based in reality or not? Whose reality?

If the other person saw the situation exactly as you do what would you say to them?

Respectfully asking someone to delve into their unseen inner world with you, as you also do, is a holy, divine, act that downright elicits courage on your behalf. Whether the person needs to take an hour, a day, or a week on the proactive questions you are asking of them to share, is okay. Simply ask that they let you know when they're ready to share their thoughts and explore the possible reason for the upset between you two. This can create a deeper bond between you two and help ensure against a conflict of a similar nature from arising again.

CHAPTER 7

Is It OK to Live in a World of *Good* and *Bad?*

❧

"I JUST EXPERIENCED RAPE."

"I just learned my sister and my boyfriend slept together at a party."

"My brother was murdered."

"I just learned I was adopted and I can't find my real parents. I'll never know who they are. They've left no trace and they don't care to find me."

The most common responses heard to statements like these are:

"I'm so sorry . . ."

"That's horrible!"

"That's so unfortunate."

"That's too bad."

Likely, you are going to see these things as really bad just like others do. But who are you or anyone else to say if a traumatic event is a strictly good or a strictly bad experience? Only God can say that. Fact is, neither you nor I know what the impact this experience will have on you or on other people. Will it inspire you to join a band of people willing to speak up and out about the reasons why nobody should succumb to the horrid PTSD aftermath of these experiences? Will the ultimate effects of your trauma fill you with a sense of purpose like you've never had before? It's possible!

Whether you are a survivor or a friend of a survivor reading this to try and understand the many levels that the trauma has affected your life or the life of your loved one, I urge you not to presume that the traumatic event, whatever it was, is exclusively negative. You haven't the slightest clue as to whether or not you or your friend or family member will see the darkness for what it was and be able to lift up and fly above it, or not. It's certainly not in anyone's best interest to put pressure on themselves or others in order to transcend the hardships caused by trauma at any one particular speed.

I urge you, as a survivor, to respond to people's polite comments, such as, *"Oh, how horrible. You must be devastated,"* with neutrality. Respond to any and all other definitive-sounding comments the same way. Do not be too quick to agree with the people who mean well when they make pitying remarks. It is incredibly key NOT to nod your head or utter the agreeing words, *"I know . . ."*

The danger of this kind of remark is that it may put you in a holding pattern. By agreeing too quickly to people's perceptions in any situation we become no more than the image of another's perception.

By accepting consolation in the form of reinforcing the obvious, you are letting other people lock you into the story of your victimization, your damage, or your loss.

Repetition of thoughts and feelings reconstructs reality in such a way that either works for you *or against you.* Therefore, instead of allowing the people around you to say things like, *"How horrible . . ."* or *"I'm sorry you got hurt . . . ,"* suggest that they try saying things like: *"I understand this is a challenge for you. I also* firmly *believe in your power to rise above this," "You're not what other people do; you are not that person's actions,"* and *"You have my permission to contact me to share whatever it is that you are going through and learning from the experience as you wish."*

We all want to thrive in this world, to make sense of the painful past in a way that allows us to move forward victoriously. This cannot be achieved individually if, as a group, we are constantly reinforcing one another's poor circumstances. Trauma is something that everybody eventually experiences in life. It's just that some of us become more at-tached to our traumas than others. It's even possible to latch on to the victor's story right away. I want that for you.

Don't believe me? I'll give you an example. I am thinking of the young American teen who was raped by several different boys older than her in the summer of 2014. One of her rapists was a teenage boy she had trusted to enjoy spending the afternoon with her one on one—or so she thought. Immediately after the rape, the girl told her mother and the police, and even went to the local news stations to tell her story to defend herself against possible retaliation as well as to protect other potential victims. Her courage was a miracle—so impressive.

We can look at our lives in an empowering way, asserting: "I experi-enced this and surely not everyone has, so I am choosing to make my life better because of it." Not for a second would my own life be as dynamic as it is today, with the wealth of experiences, adventures, and successes I've had, and the contacts I've made, if it weren't for the decision I made several years ago to heal my trauma drama and live well.

As a survivor, I urge you to make the same decision to heal and be empowered.

As a devoted friend or family member, or as a consummate healing professional, make the decision to support your loved one or client to empower him or herself.

All of us need to make the decision to stop seeing our experience through two-toned glasses. *Good* and *bad* are ideas that were forced upon us as children with still-forming brains by caregivers who wanted to help us. They taught us that we were good if we did *this,* we were bad if we did *that.* For example, some people believe that life is good if no one ever gets in your way or challenges you to stand up taller, and that life is bad if you lose control. But this approach is too simplistic.

Surely, losing a sense of who we are and what we're doing in our lives can be frightening. Also the experience of trauma is often followed by a period of aloneness. However, I do not think it is possible that the in-dividual who first said, "I am alone, not lonely," could have come to that poignant understanding with a tiara in his or her hair, or with a silver spoon that never left his or her mouth.

My point here is that we must let go of the labels good/bad for our own well-being.

Think about the collective lot of experiences someone can have for a moment. Not just your experiences or my experiences but all of the possible experiences that any one person could have. Consider the probability of these circumstances arising on any given day. Given how many possibilities there are, could we conceive of the likelihood that experiences themselves are neither good nor bad, but that each holds a world of possibility within it?

Let's imagine that a friend enters my name in the lottery (it has to be a friend since I don't usually play that kind of game) and that I win! I am elated because that means I finally get to build my transformation house, a place where people will come to learn how to shift from survivors to thrivers.

Now, let's say that my friend had put another friend's name on the ticket instead, the name of someone ascetic, living in the woods and denying himself all worldly pleasures. Winning the lottery might be perceived as a horrible occurrence by someone like that because it means the person must leave the peace of the woods, return to the city, and interrupt the new life direction to sort out the distribution of the funds. Certainly this winner does not want to be burdened by what he would see as superfluous money.

I am not for even a second denying the pain that we experience when something dreadful happens, as you most likely have deduced. I am simply advising that in the aftermath of the pain we choose to give life to our wounds, so that our negative feelings will not consume us. In fact, that's what various exercises in this book include: ways to bring life back into each of the moments within our lives. We do this by showing up to face the trouble, joust with it, connect with it, and free it from needing to come back and visit us day in and day out.

It is essential—paramount to anything else we do to heal, really—to stop viewing our experience through the lens of good or bad. We need to explore what happened internally to learn what happened to us emotionally and mentally as a byproduct of experiencing a trauma. Then, we need to examine what needs to take place in order, first, to neutralize, and then, second, to counteract the trauma's impact on us by taking life-giving actions.

It is time to write a new story.

CHAPTER 8

What Do You Do with Judgment?

❧

WHEN YOU OBSERVE THAT SOMEONE is judging you, whether your observations are made directly or indirectly, such as being told about it by another person, ask yourself this question: Do I exist *outside* of this judgment?

The answer will always be…

YES!

Reflect on *how* you exist in your life apart from the judgment of you being made by another person. This way you can take acts of judgment in stride and being judged won't crush you every time that it happens.

For example, you're at the doctor's office and the doctor attacks your weight, making negative assumptions about you and how you live your life. Fundamentally, you have two choices: You can react by defending yourself to the doctor, which is an external response, or you can respond internally through self-caring methods.

You can give yourself self-care aid in a situation like this by being aware. Practice this:

Begin by observing the focus of the individual before you. What is this person fixated on? What does her or his emotional state seem to be in this moment? And what did the emotional state seem to be when you *first* saw this person that day, week or month before you ever said anything at all?

Then ask: *How may I benefit if I detach from this individual's self-chosen current disposition, in this moment, and allow myself to be as I was before the judgment statement?*

After taking these two steps, you're in a safe place within your own self-evaluating mind, a space in which you are mentally and emotionally connected to the willpower that initiated the self-assessment in the first place. You are ready for the next question . . .

Ask: *What other parts of me exist?* (What this means, phrased in a more extended way, is: *What other parts of me exist outside of the part of me that is being judged?*)

Please be aware: The purpose of this last question is more for the awareness that it brings, then for seeking an answer or to create a long list of "parts of self" in that moment. The second we become aware that we exist outside of a judgment we are no longer bound to or attached to that judgment. This creates a sense of expansiveness *within* us and *around* us. As a result to this questioning, that expansiveness is brought to light within our *own* mind and it consequently becomes a feeling in the body. We experience this expansiveness in our minds and bodies all because we have chosen to transcend the difficulty and hardship of the particular moment.

Just because judgments are invisible to the naked eye does not mean we cannot deal with them in a practical way. We *can* get a grasp on them. We can address the emotions they bring up within us in that particular moment *without becoming absorbed by the judgments* or needing to tell everyone about what someone has judged us to be.

If we instead become fixated on a particular judgment, all that will be left will be the sting of that judgment itself.

The pain of judgment can be temporary and fleeting. The damage of believing other people's judgments can be long lasting. It is your choice which course of action you take. People may judge us, but we do not need to judge ourselves by how other people judge us. Therefore, if someone as powerful as a doctor begins to make judgments about your lifestyle and weight, or whomever else might, on whatever other topic, you can give yourself self-care on the spot and then gently, but firmly, share whatever your self-assessed, non-reactionary, *conscious response* may be. As a self-realized person, you'll understand that you cannot possibly fit everyone's perception of beauty, worthiness, and genius, thus judgments about you will not irk or trouble you. You are free by choice.

TALK TO THE SOUL

Have you ever heard of the expression, "Talk to the hand?" Well, this might actually be an invitation, in disguise, to talk to the Soul…

When someone says something to you that has the potential of injuring self-worth or self-esteem or that knowingly contributes to your trauma, I invite you to be friendly to them. In reply, try saying this, "I am sure you are well-meaning."

Even if you don't really know what their thoughts are *or even if you do know because they have told you,* the truth is their soul *is* well-meaning. Every soul comes to the planet with the intent to grow, expand, and learn in its own way and if you might acknowledge this, it is possible you will not feel compromised by what other people say to you and you will therefore perceive yourself as *more than* a victim based on someone else's thoughts and actions.

Even though we may despise someone's thoughts and actions, we can give ourselves and them the freedom to grow, learn, and expand by saying, "I know you're well-meaning." There is only *gain* for you by responding in this way. There is nothing to lose by assuming that someone means their best at their core… Just because you choose to factor in a part of them that might be well-meaning does NOT mean that you then have to have them in your life!

Perhaps by responding with, "I know you're well meaning." you *might* inspire their best. If not at this point in time, perhaps they will be inspired by your reply at another time. Whether or not you will see it, or experience it directly in them, is not the point. It is also possible that your discerning reply may NOT inspire their thoughts or actions to embody the best of intentions in the future, in this case you will still be elevated by choosing to stay out of the dumps with them!

We are each only in one another's lives for so much time. Either people will leave our lives OR they will be permanent fixtures though we may only see them but for five minutes a day, or even once every few months!

It's worth giving it to ourselves to go against the hateful or bullying methods that saturate cultures worldwide and focus instead on how we can change our lives and the lives of those *who want to change.*

I'll give you an example. A coaching client of mine visited her gynecologist. The point of the visit was to assess whether or not she was healthy after having discovered that her boyfriend was a ladies' man of incomprehensible proportions. Where he found the time in the day to flirt and pursue so many women was beyond her. She was also beside herself because of this experience of betrayal, although staying strong and focused on being proactive by tending to her personal needs and healing the emotional scars that the experience had left on her was her top priority.

The gynecologist, after keeping her waiting for nearly thirty minutes in a room by herself, came in, never smiled once, asked every question the nurse had already asked, and then began to go down the list of what she wanted to sell the woman from a bone density analysis (even though she was only twenty-five years old), to birth control pills, to you-name-it. My coaching client told her right away that all she wanted to do was check and see why she was experiencing occasional pain. Was her vagina healthy considering her partner's prolific sexual activity? The gynecologist acknowledged the statement by putting her hand up and saying, "Okay, okay; we'll get to that. First, I want to go through the lists."

Although my upset client needed acknowledgment of her pain, the gynecologist worked to fulfill her quota of dispensing meds to someone who didn't want or need them.

The feeling of dehumanization and the cold, sterile, environment that she was greeted in was the essence of a larger problem that many people call process over people. The doctor had a list of things she wanted to repeat, for a second time, even though everything was in front of her from the notes the nurse had logged thirty minutes prior. The woman who was her patient felt frustrated by the lack of genuine care. And in not being heard. She had come in for a reason and that reason had been put on the back burner in order to satisfy the doctor's protocol and system of doing things even though there was a patient in need of wholesome care.

Sometimes care is all we need.

My client reported that she remained calm and even made the point to smile. She called the doctor by her full name to acknowledge her, including the designation of "Dr."

Most of what she said either was misheard or ignored. Ignoring the voice of patients is a classic symptom of the corporatocracy of the medical world.

Upon leaving the doctor's office, my client gave herself the time to nurture herself with a lavender bath, organic foods, and a walk outdoors. She revisited the situation with me, considered, then digested, and eventually applied the "I am sure you are well-meaning" principle. The next morning, she wrote an email to the gynecologist to inquire about the meaning of a couple of the statements the doctor made only after she acknowledged, "I am sure you are well-meaning." One of those statements was when the gynecologist had said, "I can feel your ovaries because you're so skinny."

Had the doctor been listening, she would have known that her client had been ill for the past month and had significant weight-loss because of it. Instead, she blindly and emotionlessly insulted her.

With such negligent comments it is difficult to say whether or not people "mean no harm." But that is why the mantra I'm offering you here is not, "I am sure you meant no harm." We can't ever say whether or not others really mean us harm because so many people are unconscious in their day-to-day activities. When it boils down to the impact of their words they likely would defend themselves by saying, "I mean no harm."

My client intended to talk to the doctor's higher self, or soul, when she said from her soul, "I am sure you are well-meaning." The truth of the matter is that the client doesn't know how *she*, in fact, *may have triggered the doctor* just by showing how and like she naturally is. Suppose the doctor had been trying to lose ten pounds and heard from her husband every day, "Honey, you know you can benefit from doing another mile or two on your bike." In this case, when the doctor felt the patient's abdomen, perhaps she felt bad.

We don't know why people respond to us the way they do, especially when they are complete strangers. We also don't know if they intend to hurt, or not. All we know is that it takes a little bit of everyone to make a community absolutely great. And within everyone there is a part of their soul that is untouched by hatred, bigotry, small mindedness, judgments, and assumptions. I know this because all of these are mental constructs that we have been fed by our surrounding environments from the time that we were babies. Maybe our parents are saints. But we also pick up from strangers that we observed who were our day camp leaders, our school principals, and perhaps the way that the store clerk interacted with people on a painstakingly slow day.

Raise yourself up. No one else will do it for you. Talk to the soul.

CHAPTER 9

Is it Over Yet?

⌘

THERE ARE NO PERMANENT PROBLEMS in life, even though trauma may sometimes seem permanent because of the echo effects it produces in our lives. Trauma holds only the power over us that we give it. Just because it can trigger fear does not mean that we must forever live afraid.

In order to survive and thrive after trauma, it is important to accept the echos of our trauma. An echo is a memory that appears seemingly out of nowhere and its effect is to influence your thinking in ways that may not serve your highest good. An echo can lead you to disconnecting from the moment and sometimes even from yourself altogether.

By *disconnecting from yourself,* I mean disconnecting from the sensations in your body, from your rational mind, and from being able to feel anything outside of how *the memory feels.* In disconnected moments you can only feel what you felt during the traumatic event: rage, helplessness, or whatever else.

The decision to put the past behind you every time a memory of it comes up is the key to the door of healing. Sometimes we need help getting to the door and that is what this book is all about. Your healing cannot be completed if you haven't made the decision yet that each time the echo of yesterday appears you will put it behind you. It is the choice alone that is so powerful that it leads to greater awareness of the moment and greater *being* in the moment and ultimately leads to moments of change.

When we exercise the mental muscle of letting go, the subconscious will take note of it. The subconscious will acknowledge this choice as an example of what ideas, and actions you DO in fact want to fulfill you with in the present moment *and* moving forward. You can then *right away* begin to will yourself to consciously begin to search your awareness for *new* thoughts and experiences. It is the conscious action of letting go that is so exemplary of your intentions that even the details of the most looming pain will not keep a hold of you.

How to Put Echoes of the Past Behind You

A lot of life is repetition. Repetition of what you want is an essential part of the formula that leads to all successful outcomes, on all possible frontiers in our lives, including healing trauma and its possible resulting drama.

We may take actions to reinforce our decision, such as cleansing our environments of daily reminders of people, places, or events that leave a sour taste in our mouth or do not serve our highest good. If you have a displeasing physical reaction to something you see or touch, it is a sure sign that there is a memory stored in your mind-body system that is best to be forgiven and as soon as possible let go. Forgiveness is most readily experienced by NOT seeking to understand the logic of why an event happened in your life.

Why is not what we are going for.

So, how can we adjust to best serve our individual healing?

A Simple Practice

There are incredibly simple ways to begin to practice the art of letting go. For example, when I go through my clothes closet, I decide what I will or won't keep by asking this differentiating question, "Does this item of clothing hold an *experience* or a *feeling* for me?"

If an article of clothing holds an *experience*, then when I look at it I get immediate memories of where I was when I wore it and whom I was with. It retains an immediate connection to the past, but does nothing for me in the present. It doesn't supply me with any new energy, or added enthusiasm for life.

If it holds a *feeling*, then when I look at it I am automatically overcome with life-affirming energy. There aren't any memories of any particular events in my life being brought back as I look at it, just pure happiness or a sense of elegance, or whatever else that article of clothing lends.

In this process, I proactively *choose* to allow the feeling pieces to stay in my life because I want to create enough space inside me *to enjoy the present moment and the unknown moments of tomorrow!*

If I'm constantly being modeled reminders of yesterday then it's not as helpful to me in the pursuit of continuously exploring and experiencing my life in its wholeness and fullest potential.

The practice of letting go of the past by cleansing your environment is all about taking action. Action can be our saving grace when we're healing from the residual effects of trauma. Remember the power that your ability to create change gives you. Too often we can be drawn to seek affirmation of our worth and validation from others, and haphazardly forget our ability to *create* change and establish a lasting order and stability in our lives through our own actions.

BEING AT THE CENTER OF YOUR OWN LIFE

This is where I want to talk to you about experiencing yourself from within. Often, after a significant life trauma, people recollect that in the moment of the trauma the experience shifted so that it was as if they were looking at themselves and watching the experience happen as it unfolded. It is as if the experiencers of the trauma leave their physical bodies due to being in a state of shock and overwhelm. This causes them to experience the moment as an observer. It is possible that the saying, "I was beside myself" is quite literal in a soul sense.

It is certain that shifting perspectives is a defense mechanism that allows us to separate from the trauma in the moment, but if we maintain this perspective it does not serve us in the long run. As you may imagine, being a constant observer of your life is quite distanced from being in the driver's seat. If you notice that you're feeling overwhelmed or distanced from your own life, a question to ask yourself is: *Am I in the passenger seat or the driver's seat right now?*

Being detached from the moments of your life is a life-limiting effect of trauma. It is as if you are being alienated from the one person who can make lasting changes in your life: YOU.

There is nothing like the experience I'm describing. So, if your trauma did NOT include this particular experience it may be difficult to imagine or even comprehend. It is highly unlikely you will experience it now if it didn't happen in the moment of your trauma.

If you do recognize the experience as one you've had, please understand that although being alienated from one's own body is a problem *it is also far from a life sentence if you so choose.* You have the ability and inner resources to heal. Every human being, including you, deserves to be in connection to what has been yours since birth. So, what can be done when it's as if you're experiencing yourself from the outside in, so to speak? It is paramount to center your experience within yourself, again.

IMAGINE

Picture a dial before you that you're turning. You're sitting in a circle with other friendly participants of this exercise. As it's spinning, you're waiting to see where the arrow lands. Where is it pointing?

Pretend for a moment that it points to you out of everyone else who is sitting in the circle with you. How do you feel when this happens? It is YOU who is being asked to take action. YOU have been chosen to make changes, whatever that means to YOU.

In order to operate from the inside again, we must continuously recharge the core of our physical and our sensing being. We want to recharge the *connection* to being at the center of our active choice-making processes.

The only other option to *not* being at the center of your choice making is to go about living the days waiting for someone to give direction. This is pursuing how to experience life from someone else's perception and ideas of what life is all about, and it is the OPPOSITE of what is healthy.

Assuming the best, let me proceed with the eyes that you DO WANT ways to be at the forefront of your life.

Keep Imagining

One way to create a new, inner-driven dynamic in your life is to send yourself an email as the last thing you do before you get ready for bed. First thing in the morning you read it. In the subject line you say something to the effect of: "Today I feel _____because _____." (Fill in the blank with how you'd like to feel upon waking up and in the second blank what you're going to do to spur that feeling.)

Feeling is an inside job, so this is a great and simple way to get a new day started.

Another email header to send to yourself before sleep is one holding a suggestion, "Today I feel happy (or hopeful) because _____." (Fill in the blank with a reason you can believe in.)

The mind is always searching for a reason behind why we feel the way that we do. Might as well make it work in our best interest. For example, you might say, "I have due cause to feel angry right now." If you allow it to entertain this statement, without a doubt your mind will find a reason to be angry and make you angry. *Errr...*

What we may sometimes forget is that feeling is a state of flux. Our feelings change us moment to moment. And, we change our feelings. These are both natural realities.

You might say, "I feel ambitious today because _____." If you then pause to allow the mind to contemplate this statement, it *will* furnish logic explaining why feeling driven is a natural state for you.

Other email headings might be, "TODAY IS A DAY WHEN I AM SUCCESSFUL AT _____ BECAUSE _____."

"IT IS MY CHOICE TO EXPERIENCE _____ TODAY."

Over the last several years, many scientists have been researching how what we think can be literally energized into existence. The science of kinesiology is based upon the fact that our physical being is strengthened when we think life-giving thoughts. We actually feel capable of seemingly impossible things when we ponder or meditate on higher states of being that are forward moving and would benefit not only us but others.

The email exercise is simple, yet it's a great ongoing exercise to practice when we want to anchor ourselves in the experience of change in this very moment. The self that lies within us is a cornucopia of ideas, new beginnings, and adventures to be lived. It is always our own choice whether or not to connect to this great and unconquerable self.

A VISIT TO THE SUBCONSCIOUS, AGAIN

The subconscious mind is a brilliant sounding board that is constantly spinning its wheels to serve YOU. By observing your conscious mind you retrain your subconscious mind, one thought at a time. Now, that is one amazing feat. So, use these exercises to talk to your all powerful subconscious. Tame the lion by purposefully engaging it with your awareness and with your *will*.

When you are rearranging your connection to yourself so that you yourself become the most promising life asset that you can ask for in life, it is essential to remember one thing above all others: Be the final voice on your own personhood. People will tell you all sorts of grave and great things about yourself. Take everything you hear with a grain of salt and continue onward with your journey. This way, not only will you continue to experience your life from within, but you will also remain authentic. No human being can see you in your full scope. Only the Greatest Creator of All can do that!

Be the final voice on your personhood to bring assurance and satisfaction to your life. The fact that you may have been powerless during the event of your trauma does *not* say anything about who you are as a *whole* person. One second is not the whole day.

Mark Twain once said, "My life has been filled with terrible misfortunes . . . most of which never happened." I believe this statement is an invitation to keep a clear mind.

We create life as we see it.

CHAPTER 10

The Top Challenges of Trauma

☙

THERE ARE SIX CHALLENGES SURVIVORS of trauma face that cause the most trauma drama for them.

Let's look at each in turn, beginning with the challenge of trusting yourself.

THE CHALLENGE OF TRUSTING YOURSELF

After trauma, emotion often trumps logic when you're remembering. In your head, you may be asking questions such as: *What if I hadn't walked down that street? What if I hadn't gone to that restaurant that evening? Would I still have experienced the atrocity?* It's difficult for our minds to accept that we are vulnerable to injury and susceptible to other people's actions as well as to circumstances beyond our control. It is also difficult for the mind to admit that the trauma we experience says little to nothing about who we are as people. After a trauma, it can be hard to remember that we are equally as valuable, realized, and worthy as the person standing next to us who has skated through life without a nick or scrape to report to the world.

Inside, there is a balance that we must play with as we're healing from trauma: Once we trust life, can we trust ourselves? Once we trust ourselves, can we trust the world? And if we do trust ourselves and do, in fact, grow endeared to the world again, what does it look like to live within a place of trust *inside* while facing the reality that new life traumas can happen at any time? With the knowing that life is unpredictable? Each of us must find an image of life that we can trust, again, while admitting to the facts.

I suppose, in order to trust ourselves again, we must begin to trust our methods of interacting with the world around us on a daily basis. Can we change how we approach life so it is no longer the same as the way it was when we encountered our moment of trauma? If what happened, indeed, was not our fault, then can we be more prepared for danger next time?

Of course, the answers we come up with depend on the nature of the traumatic experience.

What role can we actively play as a healer? Do we need to see ourselves differently in order to gain a fresh perspective on the world around us?

If you think, *Yes, this is the key,* then where do you start?

Well, that, of course, depends on you. There are no absolutes in life. Or in this book, for that matter. Trauma is personal and even in science there is the exception to the rule. So I am asking that as we proceed you stay conscious of what does and does not apply to you. One way to go is to tackle one of the next top challenges that a survivor of trauma faces: *the challenge of forgiveness.*

THE CHALLENGE OF FORGIVING

Whether you are striving for forgiveness of self, life, or even of God, it can feel like being a prizefighter in the ring. In regard to forgiveness of the self, our own loathing over what has happened can keep us in the same fight day after day, year after year, round after round. Forgiveness itself is not always logical and often has nothing to do with the offender in the first place, but more to do with the feelings we are able to vent and express and whether or not we can eventually come to peace with the event itself. Does it mean that you will never feel anger when you think of the event, no matter who the offender was? No, you may likely have feelings because feelings are natural and part of what it means to be a normal human being. The matter of whether or not we are able to heal is what it is that we do with the feelings.

NOTE: sometimes we accidentally trick ourselves into thinking that by allowing ourselves to loathe what has happened we are paying homage to the event and the internal wounds that have come about because of the situation. For this we need forgiveness for ourselves and this mistaken thinking. Loathing the facts of our experience for too long (and only YOU know what is *too long*) is the most brutal of opponents we can face in the ring. Criticism, or loathing, of life and the self is not an act of love.

Genuine self-love is when we rock ourselves into motion again, when we cultivate our patience one more time and stand up to the changes that have occurred as a direct result of our trauma one more time. Facing both the changes that occur as consequence to the trauma *within* and *without* us.

Forgiveness involves overcoming guilt, shame, resentment, and anger that accompany any traumatic life event. You might feel guilt for making poor choices. Or shame for having been humiliated or not being stronger. Or anger that someone else's poor judgment or misbehavior has led to your past injury. We often must overcome disbelief that we were put in the situation of harm to begin with. Sometimes we must forgive people in our lives afterward for not handling our trauma in the way that we wanted them to respond, or because they spoke to us without sufficient sensitivity. That could include family members, police, doctors, counselors. It might even include forgiving ourselves. When we're hurt our nerves are raw. And without taking the time to seek answers, such as the ones found within this book, a trauma survivor can be destructive to the self, perhaps more than anyone else.

THE CHALLENGE OF LOVING AND ACCEPTING YOURSELF

It seems that when something bad happens to you, everyone, of course without meaning to, reminds you of it. If you want to learn about the almost subliminal shaming that occurs in society, due to misguided attempts at expressing care and concern, take the time to explore the work of Bréne Brown (see End Notes). When people say things like, "I'm so sorry" or "I can't imagine" an unexpected change sometimes occurs in the way that we perceive ourselves as trauma survivors. Without the proper recognition that these people are projecting their own beliefs, we can be suddenly looking in the mirror at ourselves as victims the rest of the day. Or, we're walking to our next appointment with our mind in an eerily familiar fog with memories of the moment(s) of trauma returning unexpectedly.

The problem here is that whether it is because of someone else's suggestion or because of an unconscious calling of the event on our own behalf, we are momentarily over identifying with whatever the trauma was or is. The solution is to begin with the self-love element of self-acceptance.

Self-love begins by asking questions on a regular basis, such as:

* What do I need right now?
* Where do I need to set my sights in order to both forgive the past and let it be done?
* What actions, starting small, may I take to express my approval of where life has taken me and where I am now?
* What am I willing to believe in? What people, possessing which characteristics, am I permitting to be involved in my (new) story today?
* What are the sorts of things that these people say or do to be a supporting force in my life?
* How do I feel when I'm done spending time with them?

These are all things to ponder again and again as you advance in your healing. When you come up with your answers, it is critical to act upon them. If you need a hug, ask for one. Or hug your cat or dog or a teddy bear. And always remember to *hug yourself.*

Do you know this Ralph Waldo Emerson quote? ""What lies behind us and what lies before us are tiny matters compared to what lies *within* us." Let's make this the motto of our revolutionary warrior selves. Rebel against trauma as a negative life impacter. *Let it* inspire greater love within you. The trauma is done. Refuse to let the trauma tell you how to respond to your every day. Refuse to allow it to rule your every behavior. The more we practice awareness with these exercises the better off it is that we are as total, complete, human beings.

What can you entertain within yourself today that will help you pave the way for greater self-love and self-acceptance? The answer to this question is different for everyone. Keep reading and I believe you'll find more answers—and perhaps more importantly, more questions. Healing always starts with the willingness to ask great questions.

THE CHALLENGE OF SHOWING UP IN YOUR FULLNESS

Depending on what society you live in you may be familiar with how we are told to be one or two things, but not too many things, for fear that you might outshine your neighbour, coworker, sister, or brother. I am part Canadian, so you'll believe me when I say that Canadians have a reputation for being socially minded. It's not considered good to focus much on yourself. This is why the Canadian political structure is designed so that more tax dollars go toward improving public spaces. No matter how much you have or don't have you can enjoy them and join in the fun. That's a great thing. Even the most cash-poor individual can go out and enjoy the riches of land and community space in Canada, as they are well-tended and clean.

But what if it was not monetary gain or stature that you desired? What if you wanted connection to a greater sense of self? What if your desire was to show up in the world in a way that was multifaceted, so that you celebrated how amazing you were in many different ways? What if this didn't have to detract from the happiness or glory of other people? In this book, I want to help you learn to celebrate yourself and explore many possibilities for your life. No matter what family you come from or where you are geographically in the world.

For a moment, consider that you are bigger than the meaning of the word *victim*. You have facets outside your job or career. You may be capable of seeing more than what your elders and your immediate family can see. You may be successful at accomplishing what others have told you is impossible to do. This is OK—more than OK, in fact! In fact, this is exactly what you were placed on earth to do. All of us are supposed to exceed what the people before us did. It is one of our collective purposes on this planet to excel beyond your ancestors, and what they thought they could do within their own lives. You have the best of your dad and the best of your mom *plus* the cosmic force that brought them together within *your* very being.

We can either degenerate, detracting from any progress we've made, or we can move forward and expand on the progress made by others, as well as ourselves.

Frank Sinatra didn't have the phrase "The Best Is Yet to Come" inscribed on his tombstone because it is a fallacy. He loved the Cy Coleman-Carolyn Leigh song of that name so much because of its optimism about the future. Listen to it and see for yourself what it stirs up for you.

It's Time

We sleep at night because we are meant to wake in the morning. It's as simple as that. Believing in yourself is the first step to allowing your fullest and most redeemable self to come forward. No matter what happened to you or what you have encountered in your past you have the best parts of the universe within you.

A teacher once told me that revealing our scars to people makes it possible for them to connect with us in a way they otherwise couldn't. If this is the case, then our scars truly are a blessing. They offer the possibility of connecting with others in a meaningful way that allows us to expand, grow, and be more of who we are in relationship to others.

THE CHALLENGE OF ALLOWING LIFE TO HAPPEN

Can you remember a time when you simply allowed life to happen? Of course life is always happening, but we often resist it. We get this funny idea in our heads that we have control over what does and doesn't show up in our lives. We influence the nature of what shows up by decisively taking one step or another, as well as by broadcasting this or that to the world, but just as this is true, so is the law of spontaneous combustion, or in other words, fate.

Some people think that we are predestined to experience certain events. Meaning, however much darkness or light we can each handle. Some believe that we make a pact on a soul level with the Creator, God, or our higher selves to experience whatever we do on this earth. This may be true. I myself hold this view. However, this is not to say that I am right or wrong, correct or incorrect. There are many realities in the world that coexist. This line of thought is simply what my heart personally most calls out to. I'm not here to proselytize. I am merely exploring what it takes to experience life and who is in charge of allowing that to happen. My point is this: If you are someone who believes that God is in charge and that you live by the construct of what God presents to you, then you simply need to allow yourself to be supported.

If you live by the construct that you are in a self-guided world and can make or not make anything happen, then you may wish to explore relinquishing mental control over every detail. Try relaxing your mind and watching to see if good things come your way organically.

I hope that we can all agree on this: For our well-being, we need to be open to the possibilities that are brought to us by luck, the unseen force, the Creator (or God, if you will). This means that we can give everything a try so long as it neither compromises a core value that we prize and hold dear, nor compromise one of the reasons we believe why we are here.

When I was seventeen, I was a young soul and my brain was still forming. The part of the brain that regulates risk-taking and the awareness that each risk presents a consequence was not fully developed, yet.

Science shows that up until we are at least twenty-three years old our psychology is unable to fathom that each of our actions yields an effect. We are operating off pure instinct and desire to experience the world. I had, for some time, thought that I betrayed myself at that age by seeking experiences that led to great pain even though my intent was never to hurt myself. I wanted to live in the Big Apple, but REALLY hadn't thought about how challenging that would be at that age without any contacts or real, loving, family nearby. After the traumatic experience of rape, how then might I begin to trust myself again?

How was I supposed to relinquish control enough to allow life to happen? The solution was to develop self-trust and acceptance of life through taking baby steps. It was in taking positive control of my own life, rewiring my neurological patterns, and ending the habits of being overly trusting and empathetic so that I could begin to build myself up again through cultivating my other strengths. In the deepest part of my recovery I chose to pay enough attention to myself so that I could discover new strengths *and* recover dormant ones. Then, once my esteem was rebuilt, I reentered the world from a center of positive personal power.

Up until then I had been self-effacing. I only felt I had the right to be happy to the extent that everyone around me felt happy. Before my trauma, I took responsibility for everyone's happiness by acting selflessly, to the point that I almost no longer existed. In fact, it was because of that behaviour, as well as my upbringing and it's Southern heritage, which exalts hospitality, that I wound up in trouble the one fateful night at the mafia-hosted company party that I told you about at the beginning of the book.

Allowing life to happen is a complex idea, as everyone has different ideas about what life is. What brings about life? Who's in control, anyway? As you can see, there is no right or wrong answer. However, how we decide to look at life is going to yield the answers that best suit us.

What challenges come to mind when you think about allowing life to happen, so to speak? When you know the answer to something, do you still explore and try to discover more possible answers or do you stop the search for more ways in which to experience the world? This is, after all, your world and your life. It always has been and always will be. If you feel discontented with your life, it is merely because you are either not fully owning that this is indeed yours to do with as you will. Or, it is possible that you may be unwilling to take responsibility for taking the actions necessary in order to pursue the life that you wish deeply to claim.

I invite you to believe that life is possibly open to you. Believe that it wants to be, starting now.

The Challenge of Alienation

There are many reasons why you might feel alienated if you are a survivor of traumatic life experiences: namely, the impact of shame or possibly the unwillingness to be vulnerable after the impact of your trauma. Feeling alienated from other people can be our own doing or be a by-product of social pressures, like bullying. Whatever the cause, alienation typically breeds further alienation, and more disconnection. This is why you must jump in with both feet and 100 percent commitment to eliminate this cycle.

This is the akin to the principle *like attracts like*. If we are feeling something, we will draw more of that feeling toward us because, whether we mean to or not on a conscious level, we are subconsciously looking for more of an experience when we focus on one type of experience. In this case, whether consciously or unconsciously we want to be taught something. Please read *Ask and It Is Given* by Esther Hicks and Jerry Hicks for more information on this law of the universe.

Alienating yourself intentionally is like lying on a cross and inviting a crucifixion. It's like saying, "I will willingly suffer for the experience that I've had." and "I deserve to be alone."

If we get to the place where we are unwilling to live a life where we encounter life itself on a regular, spontaneous basis we are signing ourselves up to be limited by our past. Without meaning to, we begin to grow an affinity with the misguided need to control everything.

The good news is that the moment we begin to contest this so-called need to control everything we arrive at a starting place for surviving and thriving beyond alienation and enter into a world of possibility.

The idea of safety based on control is the basis for unwanted separation from others and life itself. We need to relearn that just because we cannot control everything that happens in our lives does not mean that we cannot change our reaction to whatever is taking place.

There are so many people in this universe waiting to meet you and experience you and all your inborn gifts that possibly even you have forgotten. This coming together is best accomplished when you allow life to meet you halfway. Your willingness to engage is more than half the battle.

CHAPTER 11

Are You *Accidentally* Creating Drama in Your Life?

༽

A REALLY EXCELLENT QUESTION TO ask ourselves as a marker for whether or not we are creating unnecessary drama, or sense that we are about to create more drama in our lives, is: *Am I acting in response to unnoticed, unacknowledged, or unfelt pain?*

We must remember that drama often occurs because of unlooked at feelings concerning a past trauma. We must learn how to express our feelings, then to make peace with the feelings and let them go. Society wants this to happen quickly. We get the message: "Let go of your emotions." "Get over it already." "Let go of the experience." "Just let it go!" But that way is skipping steps in the process of healing from trauma. In order to let go, we must express, make peace, and then let go. And do you know who we need to make that happen?

We need ourselves.

That's it.

You can know for sure that self-expression is therapeutic and not toxic if, for instance, you're able to hang up the phone and walk away after saying what you felt you needed to say and forget about it afterward. Expression in such a case can help you let whatever "it" is go. On occasions like these, you will have the pleasure of knowing it's not trauma drama that's leading you to express, because you're not attached to the outcome. It is therapeutic expression if you're committed to expressing yourself and being heard, but not to marring or ruining the life of everyone who was involved with a conflict. If you do not have the luxury of having the presence of the person or people and therefore are unable to express on the telephone or in person then I suggest that you ask a trusted professional life coach, counsellor or psychologist to sit and witness you and what it is that you want to emote. The Gestalt process is a phenomenal method to facilitate this closure. Inquire with your chosen professional as to what this technique is and how it might be applicable to the healthy processing and letting go through emoting an imaginative conversation with your chosen person.

There are also other ways to nurture healthy, constructive, emoting so that eventually we can "just let it go", as some might say. For instance, after my father died I decided to write a letter to him by my own volition without having the encouragement to do so from any outside force or inspiration. After I did that, for the first time in many years my head felt lighter, my heart felt joyful. I was immediately able to focus better so that my grades soon went to almost straight As. I expressed myself to my father on paper, I made peace with my feelings and thoughts, and I eventually found the strength, courage and trust to let go.

On the other hand, if I had been caught up in trauma drama, I might have started to ruminate on how my dad could have done so many things different in his life in general, and that the human mistakes he made as a father, *that every father makes*, were unforgivable and even intentional.

Instead, the way that I expressed myself, with the intent to heal from the great loss, was therapeutic. And, that is because I chose to *consult myself* in the face of the pain I felt at the time of his loss. I took the time to confront my vast range of feelings and thoughts *proactively and responsibly (not reactively)* as a sign of respect for myself and my father's life.

That is what I want you to do when you are faced with your life challenges.

Respect for yourself is paramount in heading off drama that will potentially harm other people if you were to allow the drama to continue on or to contribute to it.

By taking a step back, *and moving into ourselves,* we observe and respect our need to process the events and exchanges that have taken place up until that point and to assess what is worth our investment of time and energy in the face of possible resolution. Remembering that there are abundant resources to have all of our needs and many of our individual desires met is key to pulling the power back within ourselves and dealing with any situation head on. We want to be more than victims or survivors. We want to eventually give ourselves the chance to thrive and that is based on the intention *and* action to continue to expand our roots in as many directions as is central to and in harmony with our core values, needs, and personal dreams.

CAN YOU PUT 'IT' DOWN?

How do you know if unnecessary drama is being created in your life based on unprocessed trauma? One great way is to assess if it's possible for you to put "it" down in this moment. Whatever "it" is, can you drop it? Whatever situation you're in that's troubling you, whatever your worry may be, are you willing and/or able to let go of the topic itself and the train of thoughts that it generates? If you cannot put it down and come back to it later, then you are caught up in a drama. And if you've been traumatized in the past, quite possibly you're caught up in a trauma drama.

If you are experiencing trauma drama, ask: *What is the root issue in this drama?*

If your thoughts concerning a specific problem or issue are of an obsessive nature and yet have no connection to deep pain or hurt within you, then your drama most likely is a self-created drama, a pseudo-drama.

If something is consuming us and we cannot get a hold of our mental or emotional selves, chances are that we won't feel satisfied in our lives. We may feel despair or there may be disrepair in relationships that you wish to cultivate and keep in your life. If we cannot get a grip on our thoughts and feelings, then it is time to intervene and use the self-regulation steps found within this book.

Another way to reduce the amount of drama in your life is to eliminate drama-prone people from your life to the best of your ability. The people who refuse to challenge their tendencies toward drama and instead consistently engage in behaviors such as blowing things out of proportion, blaming, and insulting are apt to keep you stuck in the cycle of your own trauma drama. Some people who have not experienced a deep trauma in their lives forget that there are more important things in life then to ignite drama in areas of their own and other people's lives.

Fortuitously, there are many people who have *not* experienced a severe trauma who are still amazingly sensitive to those who have experienced trauma. Such individuals are empathetically and intuitively careful not to say and do things that stir up your pain. Keep them close.

Moving forward, make a pact with the friends you decide to spend time with to find the humour in everyday circumstances and events no matter how unexpected they might be. We can't ignore that we have experiences that are disagreeable, but we *can* choose whether or not these things are going to be allowed to dominate our consciousness and lives.

Living as a Negative Result

༄

Do you know Kelly Clarkson's song, "Because of You"? From the evidence of the lyrics, we know she is singing about one person, referred to as "you," whom "she" has allowed to change the whole way that "she" leads her life. It is uncertain who the "I" is or if she is really singing about "her" own life experience, or not. The song is a great inspiration and reference point for this chapter. It points out what can happen if we take to living as a negative result. Perhaps, Clarkson gave us this song in her wisdom of what can happen if we allow other people to affect our lives to almost inconceivable proportions.

So, what does "living as a negative result" mean exactly?

We are living as a negative result if our lives are impacted by a traumatic event in a way that the effects of the trauma become more life-limiting than live-giving. In this case, the survivor becomes disoriented in life and in general unhealthy.

Remember, we always have a choice of how we respond to the people, places, and things around us. We also can develop the skill to be in charge of our minds, so our thoughts are less detrimental to our own life successes. In healing trauma drama, we are exercising our right to choose our own fate.

Clarkson's song is a great example of someone living as a negative result because it's obvious that the song is about someone who has massively altered his or her life by allowing an event that has already passed to *rule* their life choices. As I listen to the song, there is a part of me that experiences the song that wonders if the person has given up on some of the most fulfilling parts of his or her life as a way to get back at the perpetrator of the past event(s) that affected him or her so much. This false approach to so-called self-redemption, of possibly wanting to make someone else sorry for what he or she did, is as disempowering an approach as anyone might pursue.

Reducing yourself to get sympathy from someone who hurt you is not a stellar choice! In fact, it's unfulfilling and joyless.

Quietly retreating from the world for a temporary amount of time to examine our life experiences, however, such as when and if we talk to the Creator, meditate, get our hands in the soil, or walk through a preferred naturescape, can help us be more instrumental in our healing. When we choose to do these activities in which our energy is more gathered and focused, we create doorways into our subconscious minds. This happens because we are taking the time to be still and quiet with little outside noise. When we embrace more reflective activities we shift our brainwave patterns and emotional states deliberately into a calm state. We, therefore, feel more empowered and more love from the source of love itself: *ourselves.*

When we decide how many minutes or hours it is that we will pull away from external distractions and our *known* life experiences, in order to observe the moment and ourselves within it, we also ready ourselves to receive access to otherwise unknown vision and wisdom. Just as there is knowledge in books, there is wisdom in experience. Choosing your method to slow down and access your *inner guru,* so to speak, is a practiced skill.

When it is in our nature to nurture ourselves we grow and take almost unfathomable leaps within that growth.

Rather than living as a negative result of trauma, another way to be in touch with our subconscious selves is by talking to experts who have distance from the situation, training, and the objectivity to see the varying dynamics that are playing out within our lives and that are affecting our day-to-day experiences. And perhaps even limiting us without our knowing it.

When we as people take time to sit, journal about our feelings and write about what we perceive to be our most progressive thoughts in the realm of our lives at that time we can learn to see how *or if* our unrealized feelings and hurts are being manifested in negative experiences today with people who, more often than not, have nothing to do with the initial trauma or source of pain to begin with.

Until we become unaware of the impact of our most unsettling life experiences on our day-to-day behavior, we often can't understand why we are reacting to life as we are. It's therefore crucial for us to discover ways that are agreeable to us to dive in and thoroughly examine our motivations and feelings. Whether it's a solo nature stroll, journaling, cooking or planting in the backyard or in the community land plots in your urban area. Do you feel most at ease when you are in motion? If so, then closing the doors and window drapes and dancing away to your favorite music in between taking notes on your organic thoughts that arise can be a godsend when we're seeking guidance in our day-to-day.

Traditional meditation isn't for everyone. One of my past teachers, a neuroscientist in Northern California, shared a story of the time she had a client who for twenty years had been meditating although hadn't had the conviction that it was working. When she was alive, this neuroscientist offered something called the Awakened Mind Pattern testing where your brain is viewed by an electroencephalograph (EEG). Upon viewing his brain as he meditated, she observed that he in fact was in high-performance brainwaves and indeed not in the reduced brain wave state that comprises an effective meditation session. Through talking to him she realized that sitting still is not the only type of meditation that works for everyone. Her client shared that gardening kept his mind quiet and reflective. That he always felt relaxed digging in soil. So, soil became his meditation.

Meditation, then, is a single-pointed focus. It can be on whatever you want it to be. So long as you are giving your awareness to one thing as much as possible while remaining relaxed it can be anything from jewelry making to snorkeling to basket weaving to sun bathing. Be true to you and don't follow the clan.

A Word About Meditation

As a practitioner of meditation I revolt against the idea that in meditation we need to sit down and do something. I also revolt against the idea that meditation is only meditation if we are sitting and doing nothing.

The way that fundamentalists look at the world is as if there is only one way to do any given thing.

For me and, as we have just now read, many other people meditation is simply the act of holding a single focus. It you are focusing on these words and nothing else but these words right now, and all the while you are aware of your breath and yourself within the moment, by my definition you are meditating as you inwardly respond to each of these words.

Healing is an Ongoing Process

How do we face our traumas once we've journaled, taken several walks to emotionally and mentally digest, and spoken to a counselor or trauma-related life coach about what's going on? What do we do after that? Well, we apply everything we've learned and begin to create new approaches to life that feed us on every level. We need to find ways to become more gratified by life than ever before. We deserve the self-investment now more than ever and we owe it to ourselves to show our *inner selves* how great life can be, again.

Are you open to this proactive way of reassembling yourself after tough times? How open are you to finding *new* ways to live so that your life just works?

So that you're happy and eager to get up in the morning?

Since everyone's circumstances and pasts are different, most people's traumas are different, too. The exact details of the trauma are unique and how we personally experience trauma varies. Therefore, there is no panacea, no cure-all remedy, for trauma.

There is no absolute prescription in this book to teach you how to lead your life moving forward. As you can see there are lots of choices for you.

WHAT IS STRENGTH?

In their healing, some people need to exercise more of the traditional expression of strength while some people need to embody strength as yielding more, surrendering more...or allowing more. *At different stages of life and healing, both are needed for each individual.*

Expressing strength in the face of healing trauma for some means getting up again, without wasting a minute of their lives, and showing only the best of themselves to the world. For some, surrendering is the greatest strength you can know in that moment and it can mean letting go of how you feel you "should" be in any one moment and letting go of how you appear *to others* in the world throughout the process of your healing. When you surrender you are instead 100 percent based in the truth of *your* experience. You are listening to your *inner* needs. Neither one is better than the other. Neither right nor wrong. They are both equally as beneficial states to live within depending on the times and depending on individual circumstances.

There are a variety of ideas in this book that you can access whenever you want, explore at your leisure, experiment with and try on new methodology for size each and every day, to find out which remedies fit with you.

This book is written to be read over and over. I wrote it because I myself have pondered the topics I address in it over the last fourteen years of my life since I left New York. In order to accelerate my healing, I've consulted with various people around the world and noticed how my interactions with them have either positively or negatively impacted my efforts. My goal was to heal and thrive in every area of my life.

The allowing of myself to be introspective is the kind of strength that allowed me to delve inward and deep. The bringing it to you on these pages is the kind of strength that is expressive and yang in nature. Both are necessary for healing.

What about you: *How can you experience your strength inwardly and how can you express it outwardly?*

If you are someone who is grateful for all the different lessons that you've been so fortunate to receive from others and yet you see a missing hole in the information available to people, then I encourage you, first, to consider what's here deeply and thoughtfully, and, second, to go forth and offer up something of equal or greater value to your near and far away communities alike. Express your strength by serving communities comprised of people who have experienced similar life events such as yours.

No one has all the answers for everyone. It is important to share your voice and equally as important that you share your journey, whether you simply speak to your friends and family, to your immediate community, or go beyond those circles.

CHAPTER 13

"How Can I Help?"

SEEING AS TRAUMA IS A UNIVERSAL REALITY and has impact on everyone on the planet, we are never the only ones who are experiencing it at any given time. Therefore, it is great to think of others who are experiencing traumatic life events, too.

When you know someone else who is hurting, there are behaviours that, when done with awareness, can be helpful. When I say *awareness*, I mean awareness of the trauma, what exactly has happened, as well as awareness of the effects that that trauma has had.

Sometimes people don't know how they've been affected by trauma so the best service we can offer, as a loving observer, is to acknowledge the differences that we've seen in them since they were hurt. For instance, if they used to like loud events, such as concerts and sporting events, but you've noticed that they don't accept any of your invites to do that kind of stuff anymore, then acknowledge the shift they've made and invite them to go to the closest nature destination or park, a quieter, more peaceful environment that you can enjoy in together. If your friend used to get high levels of enjoyment by sticking out in the crowd and laughing and talking boisterously, but lately has been quieter, then it might be helpful to invite your friend to share activities with you where you can talk lower together.

Granted, it can be really challenging to be around a friend or family member who has changed his or her behaviour. However, in all honesty, it is an opportunity for you to grow together. Your loved one is the same as before, although they may not have the exact same disposition that you knew and connected with before their trauma.

More times than not, people will return to the lively, carefree version of themselves once they're met *where they are,* right now, as they're healing. The key here is not to try and change them once you've noticed that their behaviours have changed. Instead, showing curiosity about their healing process helps draw them (or perhaps the right word is *us)* out of the shadows of the traumatic experience, by helping us heal the shame around that experience and perhaps even get over any denial that it has in fact happened. Being a friend and loved one and not knowing exactly how to help can be a source of your own shame and guilt. So as we can see, trauma does not just impact the person who has had the experience.

Finding ways to invite your loved ones to talk, without force or expectation, but instead with the healthy anticipation of becoming closer through the experience, is the key. Anticipation is a much different angle than expectation. If we expect people to be as they always were, loud and boisterous, outgoing and unaffected on any level, we can accidentally facilitate further shame and self-denial within the survivor. By acknowledging how they want to act and how they want to feel and move about their day and honoring it by joining them you foster a sense of ease and self-acceptance within them, again. That allowing people to be as they are grants them the self-confidence, esteem and worth to overcome their challenges. Without changing who *you* are, you can still show up for your loved one who is a recent survivor of life's trauma for an hour or two at a time to meet them *where they are.*

If you are a dog person think about it like this: Would you rather deal with your dog when it is barking at you and expecting you to do as it is wanting you to do or might you be more drawn to your dog when it is wagging its tail with wide-eyed anticipation of your presence, attention, and love?

Holding space for people by allowing them to be as they are, *as well as where they are in their healing,* is the ultimate dedication to being a helper. Sometimes the shadow of trauma is so big that people lose sight of what's before them and even what's occurring in the moment that they're in.

Keep it Simple!

Trauma is destabilizing, hence the dissociation that evolves within people's day-to-day life experience when they've undergone a trauma. Keeping hangouts and visits S-I-M-P-L-E is of utmost importance. Remember that trauma is overwhelming, so whatever support and ease you can introduce into your time spent with your loved one is significant. Holding the intent to connect more with the immediate environment around you is a great act of service and love. If doesn't always need to be flashy lights and smiles to have fun, be entertained, and enjoy quality time together.

Reconnecting to life *in the now,* and with the new experience of life itself that your loved one is discovering for the first time is of paramount importance.

Remember, this can be an awakening for everyone involved. Trauma can be, and is when approached with the right sensitivity and curiosity, a call to awaken all on its own.

As you practice reconnecting with your loved one at such an important time make sure to request awareness of the new parameters of conversation. For instance, if one of their nearest dearest friends died in a car crash, you do not what to talk about your dream to go race car driving that weekend. Or perhaps the mistake will be less obvious than that. Let's say that the friend you want to comfort was once restricted from leaving an area by the limiting force of another, then reciting your experience of being on an airport shuttle earlier in the week and it unexpectedly stopping and the doors not opening and how freaked out you were is NOT a stellar idea. Save that story of being "held hostage" and helpless by the airline for another friend or loved one.

Does all this consideration seem restrictive? Well, it's not. When you truly and deeply care for someone, then making a commitment to being in the moment and present *to new levels* with another is an opportunity to enhance not only that person's life but *your* life, too. No one is "perfect" in their efforts, the survivor in your life will feel your best intent and that is what matters most above all else.

Life is a journey, and when we accept where others are and what they're going through, then we are giving ourselves the unseen gift of growth, greater knowledge of life, and greater life experience. All of which will help us in future days if and when the going gets tough for ourselves or another loved one.

Long story short: Consider asking to speak with your friend and request to know what *your friend* wants to skip over in your chats. This shows your devotion and support, allows your friend to talk, and diminishes the possibility of *assuming* what the conversational boundaries are or are not.

CHAPTER 14

Embracing the Pause

༙

PAUSING IS AN ART. PAUSE to watch the sunset or sunrise. Pause to observe the room around you instead of becoming entirely wound up in it and your surroundings. Pause to garner a sense that *you are in control* of your own experience. *Pause to breathe.*

We may accompany our pause with a focus that is either inward or outward. It is necessary to pull our power back into ourselves. And there is great power in experiencing our lives from our center which is what a pause facilitates. Pausing enables us to be on our own time, to move to the rhythm of our own drums, to determine when we will begin the next stage of our healing journey and when we will stop doing something that no longer serves us.

Even when someone is asking you to do a beneficial exercise, if you feel as if you're being pressed, you can pause. Say, "I will, *in a few breaths."* Then breathe. This helps remind the person who is making requests or expecting demands that you have inner rhythms that exist inside you outside of them.

That one sentence can be a real game changer. It's a passage leading away from victim thinking, where you might be inclined to say, "Leave me alone," to a place that says, "I see you and I honour you as a parallel to how I also honour myself."

The moment belongs to all of us, whereas your breath is experienced only by you. As you time your life by your own natural internal rhythms, the universe begins to listen and take note of you in greater ways than ever before. You give yourself the chance to be empowered.

CHAPTER 15

Learning to Live the Experience

༄

FEEL BETTER NOT BY LOOKING to feel any better than you do now, but instead by claiming, "This is my experience right now" and "Every experience is worth feeling." By doing this, you will come to a place of acceptance and further enlightenment about your own experience than you had before.

As an example, I was able to come to the place of acceptance of the idea: "Rape is not a *sexy* topic, but it doesn't make me any less sexy to talk about it. Therefore, I can let go of the fear attached to doing so." After that I discovered that I, along with a number of others in this world, was able to volunteer myself to serving the cause that I had been initiated into, so to speak. Because of my trauma, I could help others heal from their traumas.

If I learned to *live the experience,* so can you.

CHAPTER 16

Chill the Frick Out, Self-Punishment: Finding Your Turning Point

༉

YOUR PERSONAL GROWTH WILL NEVER make the leaps and bounds you might be hoping for if you're still punishing yourself for something you had no control over in the past. In fact, self-punishment may be a crutch that secretly enables you *not to feel.*

Having formerly lived my life from the outside-in, constantly seeking to determine what I was meant to do by watching for cues and wishes from other people, I realized that I would not be able to appease *everyone.* Feeling tired all the time and lacking vital life force was how I realized that I was punishing myself without knowing it and that I needed to begin listening to my *own* inner voice.

If you are seeking for an almost-mythological person to show you how to live your life then this is the perfect way to punish yourself. Or, not. *It's your choice.*

As an eighteen-year-old it seemed evident to me "that I didn't know how to live right" because I had "failed to make it on my own" a year prior in New York City. That belief is where most of the pain, the life strain, and the battles within me began. I felt as if I needed to fix the "fact" that "I" messed up my first big opportunity in life. I wanted to fix it, but I didn't know how to. As a result, I began punishing myself. My subconscious form of self-punishment was to enroll others to make me great: I sought validation from outside sources.

Thankfully, when nineteen rolled around, the desire for me to get back to my life *and let go of the power I had given others* freed me from this cycle of self-punishment. I took up yoga in the nearby park with a small group of people, found a witty and fun walking partner, started reading inspiring books packed full of wisdom, such as *The Soul of Rumi,* and embraced the courage I found deep within myself to take my first writing class in Big Sur.

It's because I started to focus on the horizon that fresh ideas to try out life *in new ways* began to come to me in truckloads! It became OK to me that my experience of rape had changed my life course away from the prestigious acting school *because I held steadfast to the idea that we are quite possibly the best thing that ever happened to ourselves.*

Whereas, just a year prior, I had been boiling under my skin from not being heard (*I wonder why!* I had been too busy seeking everyone else's opinions and advice!) I now had a greater sense of purpose and passion in life.

Can you see how these previous perceptions limited my life?

And how language choices further aggravate self-punishment?

"I want to be heard." "Why won't anybody listen to me?!" were in the foreground of my conscious thought at that time. What I realized through compassionate assessment of my own thoughts was that *they weren't real.* The thoughts and perceptions were put together by my reaction to what was happening in my subconscious: without being fully aware of it the victim of rape was still screaming to be heard, screaming to be recognized and honoured by the perpetrator who hadn't listened many months before.

The only way that I was able to reclaim myself and stop punishing myself by seeking opinions from outside people who were miniature-replicas of the rapist himself *and start listening to what I really wanted to do and experience on this earth* was to stop the cycle.

Talk about trauma drama!

Self-punishment has GOT TO GO!

Moral of the Story: Love and encouragement of ourselves are the pre-requisite steps that lead to the breaking of the terrible patterns of self-punishment that accompany post-trauma.

CHAPTER 17

My Pet Store Realization

❧

"OHHH . . . SHE'S a rescue . . ." An expression of pity swept across the pet store shoppers' faces, as if something irreversible happened to my dog, Maya, when I told them she had been abused by one of her previous caretakers.

This phenomenon brought me to a realization **that is essential for you to know before going any further in reading this book** that it is how people and things are interacted with *over time* that changes them, not one measly moment alone. You do not have to define yourself by your moment or moments of trauma. You will benefit from treating yourself well on a regular basis. Everybody does. We also benefit in our relationships and society by reconsidering how we react to people who have been abused or injured whether it be sexually, physically, mentally, or emotionally. So always be kind to others, too, as you never know what kind of traumas they are healing from.

I am now inviting you to treat the effects of the trauma that you experienced as a byproduct of that experience *and not the end product.*

When we treat the effects of trauma *as a byproduct* of someone's experience, including our own, compassion is warranted. At the very least, understanding is created. By contrast, if and when the effects of trauma are treated *as an end product* of that person's experience it's like handing a death sentence to the person who has been on the receiving end of abuse. Even more so if assumptions are made and you use the few facts you know to develop a false sense of knowing that individual before you really have been given the opportunity to get to know them.

Be mindful that you do not use the story of your trauma to define your identity. *Or, anyone else's.*

Additional resources, free podcasts with international experts and information about the seven-week online support program may be found at www.DiscoverYourResilience.Com

PART TWO

Gathering Your Tools
Prepare for Transformation

❧

CHAPTER 18

You Make the Call

❧

YEARS AGO, I WAS INSPIRED by Peter A. Levine's book on healing trauma, *Waking the Tiger*. One of the important ideas I understood from it was that there are three possible outcomes when faced with a threatening experience: fight, flight, or freeze. The latter outcome is a non-choice. In fact, a part of the unconscious mind decides on which of the three it is meant to choose based on how prepared it believes you to be to handle the adverse situation. At the time of great crisis the conscious mind has no say because a part of the brain is already accessing the situation "and making up its mind" about the situation!

It just goes to show us what complex beings we are!

The even more amazing thing about this phenomenon is that in the event that you DO freeze in the midst of a crisis, *against your own conscious will,* it is that much likely that you will be affected by the adverse effects of trauma also known as PTSD. I think this has a lot to do with the fact that we are angry at ourselves because we couldn't stop the event from happening and ashamed that we were powerless in that moment. Even though this is the case for so many trauma survivors, I must point out my strong belief and experience proving that the life-limiting effects of traumatic events do not have to become a life sentence for us if they are approached and worked through in the ways described within this book.

In the stages of my healing, reading Levine's book was an omen and Godsend. The book showed me that although my consciousness at that time co-created the experience of rape, the fact that I had been unable to physically fight off my attacker because I had frozen during that moment was not my fault. Or, my doing. If you have experienced any form of physical violation that you were unable to stop, please be aware that it was, in fact, an isolated part of your brain that was deciding for you on the spur of the moment whether or not you were capable of fighting back or fleeing. Freezing is not a weakness. It is what some of the smartest and strongest creatures on earth do in order to promise the experience of life again *after* the trauma. It is the unconscious choice to try and get through that moment by "playing dead" so that the attacker does not try and do worse, such as ending your life completely in an act of irreversible murder. If you are still here it is because you are meant to be here.

As I read *Waking the Tiger* I had another insight that the experience of trauma, which in my case involved the inability to physically move, actually becomes stored in the nervous system afterward, as a stagnant energy. In my case, the energy that was imprinted in my body-mind system was of the rage that had been felt, yet unexpressed, in the moment of my attack for fear of having my life brought to an end if I had done so. I experienced the state of constriction rather than having the freedom to move. None of these emotions, energies, and physical sensations had the chance to be expressed *because fear and the state of being frozen were dominant in my experience.*

Think about an animal that is ambushed by a member of a more dominant species. It plays dead, so to speak. That reaction of freezing when you're outnumbered or overpowered is an unconscious reaction produced by an instinctual part of our brain that is not in communication with the rational mind. As a result, fear and rage are often stored inside the muscles, organs and nervous system.

Imagine for a moment that our post-trauma emotional triggers poke and prod that energy and the feelings stored so that they come flooding back each time you are in a situation that is remotely like the experience of your trauma. In my experience, it can be terrifying and disconcerting when this happens. For the sake of clarity only, I share the following story. As you read please store feelings of *empathy* and *compassion*, rather than sympathy or pity.

For eight years I lived in Vancouver, Canada, and for many of those years I called the mountains of Vancouver home. I lived on a street named Canyon near a community known as Edgemont. I would SkyTrain and bus home from Vancouver to the mountains after teaching my healing and empowerment classes for the day. One night much like every other night, I rang the bell to get off at the stop where I was meant to get off near the street light lamp post. Exiting near the light was crucial, as there were black bears crawling all around that area. I my case, light could be a saving grace. Preparing to get off the bus, I stood at the two-stair platform near the back door, looking down and ready to step out, only the bus doors were uncharacteristically not opening. I called out, "Driver, please open the back doors!"

"Step down on the platform!" he answered curtly.

"Um, I am standing on the platform. It's not opening!" I was scared because I was the only person left on the bus other than him.

He began to drive away.

"Sir, I need to be let off! I live here!" I rang the bell, again.

The driver stopped the bus. Then he came back, stood inches from my nose, and yelled at me . . . about what I wasn't sure. It was frightening to be in the dark with only him and me standing there. After he finished his rant (about what I still do not know to this day), he walked down the two stairs himself and forced the back doors open manually.

I was scared senseless because the experience mirrored the trauma of when I was kidnapped and raped at seventeen. On that occasion I had been brought to an apartment I could not leave. I went into shock. My mind couldn't make sense of what was occurring. My body froze and felt like it belonged to someone else. I lay frozen until the wee hours of the morning. Then, when the first light came, I went to the attacker and asked to leave in a quiet, defeated voice. He sat quietly staring at me before saying, "OK, here have some cab money." He hesitated for a moment, "I wouldn't tell anyone about this if I were you." Mortified and disgusted, I declined his money. I felt confused and ashamed to have been treated as I had by someone I didn't know and would never know.

Flash forward to the night in the mountains. After a day of teaching healing classes in downtown Vancouver, this driver's behavior was a trigger for me. The interaction dug into, and deeply prodded my greatest fear and hurt. My nervous system got fired up as a result. My mind was in dread and my body was overstimulated to the same degree it would have been had I been forced to leap off a train at full speed because no one would put the brakes on.

Notice in this description that I own how I felt on all levels. There is no name calling or blaming. It is a step-by-step recollection of exactly what happened. Even the rape is referred to as an experience. Not as an event that forever made me victim to a mean, mean world.

That is a choice made by me.

People every day somewhere around the world go through similar experiences. It is disgraceful to those people only if they take it as a personal affront. This driver would have been rude to any passenger. I just happened to be the one for whom the doors got stuck.

So, what can we do when our body-mind is being overstimulated by triggers that tap into our past trauma? We take responsible action. We breathe. We wait for things to shift and do our best to iron them out.

I diffused the bus driver's verbal attack and physically invasive behavior as he stood two inches from me by not mirroring his behavior while calming repeating my harmless intention, "I want to get off the bus." I didn't react to his confining me on the bus instead of simply opening the stuck door for me other than to repeat this free-will intention. I wanted to get off the bus. I did my best not to take the driver's rant personally.

Maintaining Equilibrium

The point here is to recognize when we are jostled, *as quickly as possible*. Each time we are knocked out of equilibrium or taken aback by another person's reactions to events and circumstances it's important for us to become aware of the danger of our own reactions. The more watchful we become of our reactions to people's behavior, the more we can *choicefully* respond, and the less time we spend stuck in fruitless reaction. *Awareness* that we are triggered empowers us with the capability to respond wisely and not react like a victim. It is wise and powerful to use recognition of *ourselves* in the moment to shift gears so we may pick ourselves back up again and take positive, life-preserving, or life-nurturing actions.

Confucius is quoted as saying, *"Our greatest glory is not in never falling, but in rising every time we fall."* We can't rise if we're holding someone else back. The way we choose to respond *versus react* is the marker as to whether or not we are being responsible for our lives. If you want to be further inspired by how to take responsible actions read Mel H. Abraham's book *Entrepreneur's Solution*. The book is about far more than starting your own business. It's about finding purpose in our lives to keep us moving forward.

As trauma survivors we are 100 percent capable of shortening the time frame that we relapse into being triggered, reactive, non-productive human beings. In this state of reactivity we are not in a place to give anything back to the world around us that we feel good about in a long-lasting way. On the flip side, as we learn to respond to people in an introspective manner we regain our positive personal power and become the embodiment of realized intention that serves the greatest potentiality within the self and those around us.

With practice, we can *deeply* know mindful connection so that we may continuously grow, learn, engage, and take our stands with truth in our hearts. In the event that people may not appreciate your truth, it can still be said with the power of kindness *without expectation of any one particular response from that person.* Anticipate what you will feel from courageously remaining in alignment with your truth, instead of expecting any one kind of reaction or response from another.

RESPONDING

I walked home quietly after I was liberated from the bus, singing to a tune I had made up in order to let the bears in the area know that I was not planning to be fresh kill anytime soon. I arrived home, poured myself a glass of water to cleanse myself, and then picked up the phone to call the local bus company. I asked that they look into the experience I had that night to the best of their ability as soon as possible.

Picking up the phone was the challenge. It felt as if I was going face to face with a monster and saying, *"I will stick up for myself."* And yet do so in a *calm, non-defensive, clear* tone. Following through with doing my part to protect myself in the future from this hostile driver took a self-directed pep talk. But, I knew that standing up for myself would give both my conscious and unconscious mind the confidence that I am capable of standing up for myself in tough situations that may possibly arise in the future. Every act of self-love and every bit of strength-building matters in the face of rebuilding the healthy self post-trauma. Every opportunity to express self-love is sacred and a right of passage for the trauma survivor: you must love yourself in new and bold ways to manage through tough times.

LOOKING BACK TO LOOK FORWARD

My mother once gave me sage advice, "The first person to lose their temper loses." Plain and simple. Hands down. And something to aspire to abiding by as often as we can conjure the strength and self-will to face the task.

I was grateful that despite the rate of my heartbeat and how short my breath was I stayed put as the phone rang and the line connected. Although my teenage life had been threatened had I told anyone years earlier, in this situation I was able to take action and play my part in reporting the physical trapping that occurred that evening on the bus ride home. It is never too late to master the effects of trauma. The effects will keep coming up until we agree to work on them in the moment of their appearance.

Thankfully, the person on the other line couldn't have been more empathetic in their assurance that the union would look into it and give the driver a warning the next morning.

It is because of uncanny events like these that I truly believe we, as trauma survivors, are being given chances to make amends, stand up and heal, on a routine basis, within the effects of our traumas.

Although the driver had refused to open the bus door and instead took his verbal anger out on a passenger, I still got away without further violation. Thanks to the event, my body was able to free itself of some of the stagnant energy of fear and inaction that had been previously stored in my nervous system from years prior.

Nothing is all good. Nothing is all bad...

Because I had taken the opportunity to stand up for myself, I felt a sense of empowerment and relief.

In future days, I learned that taking martial arts, where participants are asked to kick and scream, is also a fantastic, nonviolent way to breathe the body free of pent-up, stagnant, feelings and energy. If you've never looked into martial arts, consider doing so.

The teacher will love your enthusiasm.

Tennis is also a great way to *"whack"* that frustration out of you. Every time you hit the ball imagine freeing yourself of stuck, old, energy that no longer serves. Private tennis lessons where no one is expecting you to win are great for this. Or, go and get a used tennis racket and find a wall.

Bottom line: When we shrink back from an experience, we draw all the energy of that experience into us without meaning to.

Energetically shrinking back is the equivalent to emotionally holding on to feelings and not expressing them.

If we do this, we suffer. No one else.

On the contrary, when we face and stand within whatever the moment presents, the light we project by doing so disintegrates the overwhelming sense of hurt and we are graced with the wisdom and strength of the pain.

Pain Teaches Us What to Do Next

There is a difference between pain and hurt, just as there is a difference between pain and suffering. When we are hurt, we are immobilized. It is often because we are focusing on the hurt as the single-pointed focus of the moment that it warns to consume us in the form of ongoing suffering.

Psychological pain is an awareness that occurs when we remain open to a traumatic moment and all that is happening within that moment. When we shrink back from pain by denying its existence we create the experience of prolonged hurt. However, we are capable of continuing to move within the parameters of our lives while keeping our eyes on the horizon *if* we allow ourselves to feel pain instead of pushing it away.

The dynamic between yourself and optional choice of suffering is like what happens if you hurt a limb of your body. After a traumatic experience we can move on emotionally once the initial hurt upon impact has been done if we are not removed from it. If there is a safe enough and accepting enough environment to process and digest the experience then we can come in touch with the hurt. This way we do not remain traumatized for life.

Take a Pause. . .

Let's take a pause for a second to ask how you can foster an environment where one to two hours a day you can be with what it is you are experiencing in its full breadth. Where you can come in contact with everything that is occurring as your internal experience and truth. That's what this book is all about: give yourself time to sit with whatever it is that you are experiencing and take notes as you read this. Notes that perhaps only make sense to you. So, that you can deepen the connection to the process of your emotional and mental mending of fences. The deeper we allow ourselves to go the more powerful this is. If you live in a household where you do not feel emotionally safe from criticism for how you are choosing to deal with and process the events of your lives then the idea to take notes with keywords that

perhaps only make sense to you but that ignite a reminder of what it is that you are intending to remember from these chapters then THAT IS GREAT!

If we mentally focus on the incident of the trauma over and over, without the intent to change our perception of it, then we are literally harming ourselves by impacting our lives over and over, as we re-experience it over and over, with each and every recounting of the event. Doing this hurts the present and limits the future. Choosing *how* we focus on the past and giving thought power and energy to actions that *move us forward* help relieve any unnecessary residual pain from an initial hurt.

Suffering is optional, whereas with pain we have zero control. Pain is simply part of the experience of being human. So is being vulnerable. And we are not truly alive if we are not open to being vulnerable from day to day. In fact, we experience more pain and suffering bottled up in a protective sheath to block ourselves from possible hurt rather than if we simply embrace the experience of pain. If we allow ourselves to feel pain we are more prone to being reflective in general, and more likely to be gentle with ourselves...and are therefore kinder to others.

Think about it like this: If I break up with my boyfriend, it is my choice whether or not I suffer. The pain of the loss is inevitable because someone I love is no longer in my life in the capacity that I once wanted him to be. On the flip side, focusing on the loss day in and day out and therefore consequently neglecting other aspects of my life and *creating suffering* is optional. I have the power to say, *"I am in pain and I am choosing to move through my day in service to my community and my highest purpose."*

The World as Healer

After an initially horrific event, *any human* may be in shock. At such a time, going back to work right away to serve is not advantageous. However, as your nervous system comes out of shock, making a pact with yourself to take one small step a day that enables you to contribute to the community is essential for the soul's recovery. No matter how horrible the world may have seemed during the time of the trauma experience, a key of healing is to think beyond the parameters of you alone.

What constitutes service or making a contribution to the community? It doesn't have to be anything monumental. You might start a blog about what you experienced and what you're learning, for instance, to share with chosen friends and/or family. That could help you make a great leap toward your personalized recovery. A very safe way to share only with precise people you choose is to set up a Google Drive document and issue invitations to view it to a limited few. Another way to help yourself move through the pain of a trauma or manage the post-traumatic symptoms of being triggered is to do a daily meditation. Meditations can last anywhere from five minutes to thirty minutes or go beyond. It is true that the mind clears itself more the longer you are in meditation, however, five minutes of time carved out just for you is also a treat that is worth giving.

I often ask myself, *"If I don't show up for myself then who will?"*

Show up for yourself and others will, too. And often in new and subtle yet astonishing ways . . . ways that make a WHOLE lot of sense *to you* and *your* unique innermost self.

Daily Affirmation
The resistance of the Universe is our assistance
to remember to stand taller, live bolder,
and be stronger.

CHAPTER 19

Affirmations

❧

IF LOVE IS A HEALER, then what can we do to attract more love? The answer to this seems to be the creation and application of as many new and profoundly loving thoughts as possible in any given day. Since this can take a lot of time and personal energy, energy that the trauma survivor does not always have access to at the begin stages of healing, I have given you sample affirmations at the end of this chapter to start with. An effective way to reshape our lives is with affirmative thoughts which are statements asserting that something is true even though we may still need to grow into them before they are realized in their full potential within our lives. We direct our thoughts where we want our lives to go even though we are still on the road to getting there.

The conception of an affirmation can only take place once we are aware of our thoughts in the present moment. Perhaps where we are within our minds is a far cry from where we want to be, and yet realizing this distinction can be our first key to shifting to the next 'level', if you will, of thought. Affirmations, for instance, are always spoken from a positive standpoint. Instead of saying, "I don't want to feel ugly anymore," you say, "I want to, and now allow myself to, begin focusing on my strengths, including my physical, mental, and emotional strengths—for each of these amount to my feeling and *being* truly beautiful inside and out."

An affirmation is always life-giving in the most positive of senses: It allows us to grow and evolve beyond past limitations. Affirmations are most effective, in fact, when imagining where you want to go next within your life and projecting the words of the affirmation with as much enthusiasm and purposeful belief as you can muster in each and every moment that you are practicing them.

Affirmations are to be said on a regular basis until there is no longer any more internal resistance when you are speaking them, whether you are doing so silently or aloud. If you feel resistance as you choose the new thought that you imagine is a potential catalyst for your self-growth, please understand that this is a natural and temporary response to a new idea that is not currently engrained in your subconscious mind patterns. But just because you do not believe a thought now does not mean that it is not worth incorporating into the future, yes?

Did you know that statistics show that most people think the same thoughts every single day of their lives? This is true. Can you imagine *that by not imagining* or setting our sights to the horizon in the mind space of possibility what this is doing to our spirits, our lives, our relationships and our evolution as a multi-dynamic species? I'm sure you can, however, I prefer for you not to think *too long* and hard about this beyond the realization of this very fact. Life either improves or degrades as a result of what kind of questions it is that we contemplate! So, I'll call myself out: That is a terrible question to over invest in and yet I notice all the time that many of my clients focus and wonder too often about perspectives that do not enhance their lives one bit!

So here goes on some affirmations that we can apply to our lives. You may simply read them or you may also turn on a recording device, something as simple, free, and accessible as an iPhone or smartphone before recording what you read and playing it back to yourself in the morning and evening.

If you prefer to have a friend speak these affirmations for you, or perhaps a guide or counselor whom you hold in high standing, and whose voice you find encouraging, please ask them if they will help you to make affirmations a part of your day and/or evening. Explain to your friend that you want to be proactive in your healing and you desire a little bit of help. You can always return the favor!

Sometimes a significant other or very close family member, or even a friend, is not the best person to ask. The reason why this may be the case is that these people already play such a significant role in our lives, being a much loved friend or family member, that integrating another monumental role in your life could cause a blurring of boundaries for them. Only you can be the judge of who is appropriate to ask for assistance. The best support is neutral.

There are no absolutes, of course, so if you have a beloved sister or brother, or a dear friend who you share a therapeutic relationship with, or a parent whose voice you want to hear affirming powerful healing thoughts with you every morning and evening, then go with that. Always go with your gut.

Play with the following affirmations: recite them exactly as they are or reshape them to best fit your life.

I accept and honor myself on this continuous life journey of giving and receiving love.

My love needs to be continuously spoken and fulfilled by myself and others.

My heart's desires are spoken with courage and thus ease.

I take refuge in knowing that I am co-creating a steady supply of love in my life on a daily basis.

I trust in the higher powers to assure the flow of that which my heart, mind, body, and soul rejoice and delight in together.

I am open to the life-enhancing moments of my today.

I am open to the uplifting and positive ways that my life is changing.

I am aware of ways to raise my vibration, and I now do so throughout the day.

I focus on my dreams, goals, wishes, and desires on a consistent and fruitful basis.

I open to the possibility of who I am today.

I am both formless and rare in form. I am limitless and personified by that which is bright, sacred, new, and fresh.

I nurture perceptions of myself that are healthy and life giving.

I allow the love of those around me to permeate all aspects of me.

I understand that love is the frequency that allows me to reach each and every one of my dreams, goals, and aspirations. The expression of love in my life encourages me and others to be the best version of ourselves in our own time.

I am open to love in all of its many forms.

I express gratitude for the many ways that love is shown to me.

My innate desire for love is what makes the world go round.

Although love is a feeling, I also include it in my thoughts.

I realize that thoughts including the vibrations of love strengthen me and all of my relationships.

CHAPTER 20

How to Write Affirmations

❧

AN AFFIRMATION IS A SUPER-CONSCIOUS intention that may not be an entirely accurate description of your present reality right now however it is intended to be an integrated part of your reality moving forward into the unknown. Carefully constructed affirmations permit the speaker of the intention to shift from one state of being and thinking into another so that the new thought may eventually become true with a combination of *intense* belief and *fiery* desire to see *and experience* change. The purpose of an affirmation is to heighten productivity by encouraging yourself *on all levels* and reshaping your sense of self in the greatest respect.

Here are the rules to follow when creating an affirmation for your morning or evening meditation practice.

- **Remove negatives** from the writing and speaking of affirmations. For example, instead of "I am not poor anymore," you write, "I can feel myself becoming wealthier by the minute."
- **Make them "I" focused.** For example, instead of "Grandma thinks I'm smart now," say, "I know in every fibre of my being that I have what it takes to make smart choices in every aspect of my life."
- **Speak in present tense**. For example, instead of "I stopped cooking late at night," try, "I enjoy cooking at hours that still give me the time and freedom afterward to move around and healthily digest."

CHAPTER 21

How to Say Affirmations

❦

BOTH PREPARING AND BLANKLY REPEATING statements is not the same thing on an effectiveness scale as is the deciding of *how* you will embody the affirmations. Here are a couple of pointers to begin practicing as soon as possible so that you can take them on board as 100 percent fact in your newfound life!

MIRROR EXERCISE TO STRENGTHEN YOUR AFFIRMATIONS

1. Stand in front of a mirror and smile at yourself for a total of one minute. I am aware that this sounds idiotic and possibly buffoon-like *and* that's OK. The subconscious responds great to the suggestion that you like yourself enough to smile at yourself. It takes the cue on board and immediately starts to ponder, "*How can I be my own best friend today?*" Just because you cannot *see* the wheels turning does not mean that they aren't!

2. Now, in addition to the smile, *nod* your head YES as you state your first affirmation. In this case, let's use the affirmation "I see myself as whole now." So nod your head yes *while smiling* and say the affirmation in earnest.

3. Pause while continuing to smile. **Head still** for a moment. **Lips resting shut.** Take your right hand and **tap with your fingertips** *gently* on your sternum in the center of your chest. This is above

the nipple point and below the collarbone in the center of the chest. Energetically this area is known as your Higher Heart. There is a lot of power stored in this area of the body, so now as you repeat the affirmation a second time, you are smiling and tapping gently at the center of your chest.

4. Pause and take **two long inhales and two long exhales.**

5. Challenge any possible conscious *or subconscious* resistance by now placing your right hand on your left shoulder blade and your left hand on your right shoulder blade. Now squeeze so as to **give yourself a giant hug.** Continue to embrace *yourself* for two to three full breaths. *If* tears arise, honor them as part of the process.

Be courageous and give this exercise a try at your earliest opportunity.

BONUS MATERIAL

❧

Sample Affirmations

THESE AFFIRMATIONS ARE FOR YOUR use whenever you wish. You may say them in the morning right when you're waking up or in the evening after you get into bed. Storing them in the nightstand beside your bed is a great way to encourage yourself to continue practicing your affirmations and thus increase your level of belief in them. Remember that the affirmations are being said because you want to grow into them. So, don't worry if saying them doesn't seem natural when you first begin. For increased success with your affirmations, speak them during breaks throughout your day. Even record them with your smartphone or an old-fashioned tape recorder and listen to them.

If you are dedicated to these affirmations they will help to serve you to shift from survivor to thriver.

LOVING THE SURVIVOR IN ME

- Even though the person who harmed me wanted to control me in that moment, and perhaps did, I now take control over myself today and every day moving forward.
- Although I may have been helpless in the moment of the trauma, I now embrace my power in every way that I know how.

- My actions are always for my greatest well-being and therefore the well-being of everyone involved.
- As I heal myself, I heal all relationships in past, present, and future.
- I choose my well-being and realize that it is mine for the taking. Only I have the power to give it to me. Only I have the power to take it away.
- I choose the path of most love for myself.
- Although I cannot change the facts of the past, I can change the feelings related to my past, present, and future.
- Although life is unpredictable, I realize and visualize my strengths. I know I am more than capable of dealing with the moments as they come up. I choose to trust myself, again.
- The past is a mirror of my old beliefs, whether they are conscious or unconscious. I now choose to reshape my beliefs to support myself today.
- I realize that although I know a lot about my potential I also may have many capabilities that are waiting to reveal themselves once I reshape and let go of any outdated beliefs.
- It is because I know that I am now safe that I can value moments in which I am both in control and not in control.
- As frightening as the idea of letting go might be to me, I realize that it is also the state that makes the felt sense of oneness, receptivity to others and my environment, and a deepened sense of connection possible in my life.
- My life and my truth are beautiful because I allow myself to see that they are.
- I am the hero in my life who I have been waiting for all along!
- I am unstoppable in my recovery!
- I have control over the way I react to change. I make change work for me.
- No one knows me as well as I know myself.
- I choose to hold myself in high regard. I realize that although my life may have been adversely shaped by others actions in the past I now renew and redeem my power one step at a time.

Staying in the Present Moment

- I embrace this moment more than any other.
- I am happy here. I am thriving here.
- Goodbye, Anxiety! Hello, Moment!

Create Awareness of Inner Fortune

- I am grateful that I have deepened my relationship with my inner core, as this allows me to relate with all people on a genuine and connected level.
- I am grateful for having achieved the goals in my life that I *have* so far.
- I am grateful that I have found a way to equally distribute my time between rest/rejuvenation and the active embodiment of my goals.
- I am grateful that I give myself several times throughout the day to reflect on the always available priceless beauty and happiness within.
- I am grateful that I give myself at least one new experience per month.
- I am grateful for the ways that I honor my inner needs.

Affirmations for Community

- I attract people into my life who inspire me to live in alignment with my inner vision, and who encourage and support me in all ways.
- I surround myself with women and men who see at least two sides to every question, people who are open-minded and believe the very best is possible in life.
- The people around me love introducing me to their friends, who in turn help me achieve my goals.

- I am building business and social networks everywhere I go thanks to my courage, tenacity, intelligence, strength, pleasant outgoingness, and natural gifts and cultivated talents!
- My friends form a circle of love around me that uplifts me and inspires and encourages my greatest strengths to surface.
- I allow the care of those around me to permeate my being, mind, body, heart, and soul.
- I serve Spirit.
- I am deserving of love and I joyously open to it in its many forms.
- I am grateful for the vast family networks I have where unconditional love and divine, intuitive support prevail.
- I have plenty of energy to nurture my relationships.
- I value my relationships.
- I am learning to master my time. And so it is.
- I inspire people to their greatness. I am willing to embrace both the universal nature *and* unique nature of my soul.
- I have a keen interest in what happens when my consciousness meets other people's consciousness.

GEARING FOR SUCCESS

- My ability to perceive my own greatness takes me to new heights.
- My gains far outnumber my minor losses today and onward.
- My ability to implement my desires every day is free flowing and real.
- I receive universal energy from dreaming about doors opening up for me in my chosen profession.
- I trust my creative flow in my projects.
- Creative energy flows through me as I embody my chosen profession.
- I am a big dreamer grounded in my experiences and gifts.
- I am practiced and successful at saving money on a paycheck basis to achieve my stated goals.

- I spend money wisely and joyously. I receive money joyously and gratefully. I always have plenty of money!
- My chief aim is for my career and the living of my passions to provide for my financial, social, and familial needs.
- I am winning notable rewards in my chosen profession. This feels amazing! I am deserving!
- I am a big dreamer and realistically talented. I am grounded in my experiences and gifts!
- I am gaining significant and helpful clarity every day with my projects.
- My willingness to help others expands my network in the direction of my dreams, goals, and aspirations effortlessly and joyfully.
- I am moving forward with rapid speed while rooted to my deepest truths and purposes.
- Today is the gift I've been waiting for. I embrace it as such.
- I replace telling the world about what I can do with showing my community, family, and friends how capable I am.
- I have a talent that is special to me and to the world that only I can fulfill and fulfilling it I am.

Self-Healing Affirmations

- I realize that all possibilities in the universe are within me too. I am aware that I am capable of awakening any possibility in my life by going within me.
- I feel as if I'm lying in a big giant hammock that wraps me in an embrace of calm, warmth, support, and divine connection with all that exists!
- I have the techniques and power to change old habits and patterns. I now do so with love and compassion for myself.
- I live in a beautiful home and have time to do my work, socialize, and restore my vital energies to my satisfaction.

- The recognition of my strengths by myself and others creates a sense of calm within me. I lovingly validate myself in every moment.
- I value my confidence and the new places that it takes me in the world and in my relationships. I am proud of who I am and the work that I do.
- I am open to the life-enhancing moments of my today. I am open to the uplifting, positive ways that my life is changing.
- I jump for joy. I move with joy. I am full of joy!
- I am aware of the ways to raise my vibration and I now do so throughout the day!
- I open my heart to the possibility of who I am today.
- I am formless and rare in form.
- I am free of limitations.
- I am personified by that which is bright and sacred, new and fresh.
- My perceptions of myself are healthy and life giving.
- I indulge myself in all things that feel emboldening and illuminating for my soul, spirit, heart, intellect and body.
- I am connected to a divine, radiant current of energy that supplies me with the will to align with the highest creator within me and to connect to the explosive energy that makes up the entire universe for the greatest good of all.
- Creator, thank you for giving me a mind as open and unlimited as yours today.
- I have and continue to develop habits that cultivate my unique gifts and abilities.
- My beliefs match my greatest self and my greatest potential.
- I have an inventive, organized brain. The left hemisphere of my brain and the right hemisphere of my brain communicate with divine harmony to support my best thinking and decision-making processes.
- My mind is a well-tuned vehicle that takes me all the places I want to go.

- I let go of the "how" and allow.
- I bravely continue to talk about and take action on my dreams. I believe in me.
- I anchor myself in environments that feed me.
- I say affirmations with fervor in my daily spiritual activities to affirm my divine and immediate connection to the Greatest Creator of All who harmonizes with me to bring me loving, healthy results that both uplift and challenge me to new heights of community engagement and personal success.
- I owe it to myself and to community to set high standards for myself.

BUILD YOUR ENERGY

- I take time out every day to evaluate my life and my level of contentment with it.
- It is safe to be the best version of me.
- I determine the state of my well-being.
- I learn to accept other people and their actions. I therefore have an infinite amount of energy to pursue my today and all of its goals and dreams.
- The amount of energy I have is in direct proportion to how much time I invest in the things that I can change.
- More times than not, my source of energy is my willingness to live in a state of clarity.
- I allow my mind to attain clarity in all areas of my life.
- Though I may not always know the answers, I know where to look for them.
- I am fortunate that I am able to see my life as a whole: I honor the details without getting stuck within them.
- I see that one of my special powers is to forgive. My power is to learn from my past and move on from my past.

Cultivate Inner Freedom

- I peacefully live my life beyond other's desire to control me, my actions, or my thoughts.
- I am content with allowing other people to think as they think.
- I spend more thought energy in encouraging myself and other people rather than opposing myself and others.
- I recognize that everyone has her/his own patterns and thought inclinations, and I therefore choose to detach from either harmonization with another's thoughts that are not in resonance with mine as well as from thoughts that are possible sources of upset for me.
- I choose to live in happiness, health, and strength of mind.
- My will power is the greatest assistance tool that I have in this life.

Affirmations for Healthy Romance

- I am brave enough and courageous enough to face the love that I seek as I know that I am co-creating through thought and anticipation of a healthy romance.
- I am receiving the exact kind of life and love I wish for. I energize thoughts of love and the belief in my ability to effectively and compassionately give and receive love.
- I am excited about the authentic love I experience in my love-based heart.
- I accept and honor myself on my continuous journey of learning to give and receive love.
- My sexually and romantically involved partner and I continuously fulfill one another's deepest and most whimsical heart desires.
- I trust the flow of that which my heart and body delight in together within the realm of my romantic relationship.

- I love my partner with all my heart. We are completely honest with one another. We are dedicated and loyal to one another. We inspire and encourage one another's dreams and passions.
- I am a desirable partner. I find my pure magic within myself. I dazzle and entice. I am beautiful/handsome.

Please allow yourself to pause for a moment now that you're finished reading these sample affirmations for the survivor and thriver. Observe your breath. Feel your stomach move in and out. It moves out as you inhale and in as you exhale. Allow five to ten breaths of this heightened body awareness as you focus on where your breath moves most easily throughout your body and where you may want to open more to the felt sensation of your breath.

Remember, every day is a new opportunity to move in the direction that you most desire; no matter what has happened or what someone has said or done, you have the ability to change the minutiae of your life for the best version of you. One breath at a time. One step at a time. And, of course, one *thought* at a time.

CHAPTER 22

Taking Feelings on Board

༄

MANY PEOPLE IN THE WORLD live in a corporate structure that does not hold space for its employees or coworkers to express emotionality. Since many of us spend at least forty hours a week at work—never mind the often frenzied time of traveling to and from work on public transportation or in a car immersed in heavy traffic—we spend a lot more than that dedicated to routine activities that merely keep the survival end of our lives working.

The same often goes for many schools and universities that make little room for the unfiltered emotional self to recognize itself and/or express itself.

Considering the obstacles, when do we embrace this integral part of ourselves? We don't have many options if we are not in an environment that allows us to say, "Bobby, I am feeling quite happy right now, would you mind if I laughed out loud to express it?"

Conversely, if we find ourselves desiring to laugh without some-one in the room knowing why we are laughing, our behavior may be questioned.

We might hear the wrathful, *"Why* are you laughing?"

But what would happen if we lived, worked, and schooled in envi-ronments where we, as individuals, can be forthright about where we stand emotionally in order to knock our communication up to the next step on the proverbial ladder? Whether people completely understood us or not, we still have the opportunity to *be* observed *and compassionately accepted* as the whole people that we intrinsically are and were born as. We would be known in greater depth to those around us. We would be more intelligent in the face of understanding what is going on within each of our coworkers or school mates. We would be less tense and fearful of being seen in our emotionality. We might waste less time in premature self-judgment and self-preservation in the face of whether or not it is correct or OK to allow ourselves to be perceived as *full beings,* with emotional selves, in addition to being seen as our brains and our physiques.

Overall, embracing our full selves *no matter what our settings may be* might very well enrich our relationship with the *present* moment and with those around us while bolstering heightened creativity and therefore productivity in life and at work. For communication, as we know it, is a progressive experience. When it is at its best it determines whether or not we feel close to one another and are getting what we want and need from our relationships. It doesn't make any difference if these are taking place in the classroom, a workplace, or in the living room at home.

What if all within one sentence we can say to one another the emotional component of our existence combined with our left-brained logic?

It is helpful that in the expression of our feelings, the same feelings that we all share beneath the skin level, we invite the person, or people, listening *into* the experience versus dictating what we want the listener's experience or response to be. This welcomes a balance of gentleness and firmness at once. Both of which are necessary; too much of one and we break and oftentimes become disconnected from the reality of our settings and the people within them. As the Tao Te Ching says, *That which does not bend breaks."*

In fact, many people resist using feeling words when they speak to their colleagues because they fear offending them. They may be under the impression that what a speaker says will haphazardly *cause* the listeners' feelings to change.

With an open mind authentic conversation often can and does take place.

When you are the person who is taking a risk and sharing your feelings it is important that you address the situation as forthrightly as possible. It is tantamount to do your best to assure the listener that he or she is not the *cause* of the feeling word being spoken ("I feel *sad because of what I notice. I am not saying that you are doing this; I am saying that this is what I see as happening. This gives the listener the opportunity to learn of, and possibly even see your perspective without giving your view as if it is the only reality present in the situation.*")

It is best to let the listener off the hook. Using feelings to blame or position ourselves above others is a lose-lose scenario. Feelings are to create connection. If you're using them for any other reason you are creating drama.

It is a *choice* whether or not to live a life of inward *and expressed* integration of each of your soul's parts. May you have the courage to accept the individual facets that make up the *whole* that is *you*.

CHAPTER 23

Counteract Victim Talk

❧

ARE THERE USERS IN THIS world? *Of course.* The difference between the response and the reaction is that some people take on board the lesson of loving themselves more *because of the misuse of themselves* and others take on the misguided lesson that they are victims of someone else's whims. Then they over-identify with that new label: *victim.* Every experience is open to interpretation.

Only you have the ultimate influence over the narrator in your own head. As a bypasser in Los Angeles once told me over ten years ago, *"Don't let that person rent space in your head. That's valuable real estate."*

One of the major causes of drama is having triggers in a blind spot. This can result in strong reactions to the smallest provocation. Let me give you an example of how our trauma can either be our medicine or in this case the poison of self-perpetuating drama.

Being silenced was something I was familiar with as a kid. That set me up with a blind spot about the issue of being silenced. *As a young adult, I therefore would make sure I always got the last word in and that I was always given the chance to be heard.*

As we discover our triggers, we begin to develop vision in our areas of former blindness and our lives are expanded. In my own case, as I grew and had enough interactions with people who didn't take other people's feelings or individual selfhood into consideration I realized that getting the last word in was actually a disservice to me. My well-being is more aided by investing my time and energy into people who are alive in their considerateness and loving with their words, actions and ears.

I decided that I knew I had something to say and that my words are worthwhile because they help other people learn and reflect on their own lives. I realized that being heard would be my medicine. That I can find ways to be heard that assist people and their growth. And, to speak in situations where my words are anticipated. My decision to teach, coach, write and speak has been my healing balm of choice.

Whereas, I may have continued to make sure *everyone* heard me, I instead now focus on *who it benefits most* to hear me.

Sure, we as people are almost programmed for drama, but humanity is also programmed for a whole lot more.

Is it normal to be faced with drama? Yes, but it's also not normal to get *caught up* in drama to the point of making yourself and your life sick.

We run our lives. Not the other way around.

We are not victims.

The opportunities to overcome trauma drama, also known as *the unnecessary drama resulting from unprocessed trauma,* are right before each of us every day.

Will we react? Will we respond? How?

Will we catch ourselves before we start reacting so that we are giving ourselves the opportunity to respond in a way that most benefits everybody?

What are the pros of doing so?

"That's My Drama Story"

You may use the following to gravitate toward yet greater self-knowledge concerning your trauma drama inclinations so that you won't constantly be retriggering your initial trauma. When you evaluate your untended and unresolved trauma drama stories, it is best to look at the following areas.

1. The *cause* of the drama
2. The aggravated *effects* of the drama

3. The *shift* of thought aka the shift statement
4. The *story reimagined*
5. Activate *goals* to implement beginning today
6. *Future damage control methods* to prevent the continuation of the trauma drama

The purpose of this exercise is to give you tools to stop trauma and its resulting drama cycles in their tracks any time you're in distress. Once you've made the powerful observation that your mind and emotions have a tendency to go out of control, it is best to be open to redesigning your reactions. This exercise below will help you regain self-control and mental focus in temporarily challenging situations. For the sake of clarity in demonstrating this exercise, here's an example that I am using in first-person language to make it easy to follow. When you are doing this on your own, you will be reading the underlined phrases aloud and then adding the details of your own circumstances to the formula listed above in numbers one to six. Use your discretion to modify any of the words to best suit your personal journey.

When you notice yourself being reactive to your circumstances take the following steps.

Step 1: Name the source of your pain. The cause of my drama in this moment is . . . [fill in your own story]: that "my" housemate appears disgruntled, hurt, and angry after "I" have stated my physical boundaries. In detail, I have made a request that my housemate not sneak up on me from the back when I am in the kitchen. I gently told my housemate that when *anyone,* not just him/her, unpredictably walks up behind "me" I feel scared and uncomfortable. In order to connect authentically and genuinely I practiced positive vulnerability in sharing that people doing so, in general, is an unnecessary trigger for me because of the trauma in my past. As a result, my housemate is upset and consequently I am stressed.

Step 2: Observe the symptoms. The effect on me is . . . [add your list below, the following are merely samples]:

* Withdrawing from my surroundings.
* Resentment.
* Altered efficiency at work.

Step 3: Declare aloud that you are in control of your thoughts and feelings. Practice this shift statement to move from your current state to the chosen state of mind that is most empowering to you: "I can change this cycle by altering my response and saying in response to my noticed trigger, *'That's just my drama story.'* "

When you make this acknowledgement be sure to use a nonjudgmental, neutral, and factual tone.

Step 4: Reprogram your mind and reactions by reciting the following all-powerful affirmations aloud. Be sure to state these affirmations in order. Our self-told stories can be pivotal in how we may more easily access change within our lives OR life-limiting. It is our choice. We, therefore, need (and hopefully *want*) to change the stories that we choose to follow within our minds.

In order to designate this shift within ourselves say your my story reimagined affirmations. They are as follows:

"I am a warrior. I choose to see through the kind of feeling or emotion that acts as a weighted cloud versus illuminated potential."

"I am willing to transform the kind of human emotion that is paralyzing."

"I am allowing myself to *shift* so that my mental and emotional selves are life-enhancing in the most positive sense and so that I may make the changes that I both need *and* want."

"I choose to give life to thoughts, mental states, feelings, and actions that grant me the freedom to continue on my journey to learn and grow."

"I let go of my old pattern to unconsciously attach myself to immobilized states."

"These thoughts are gatekeepers of change and are here for me to return to whenever I wish."

Step 5: Set goals for the new way you wish for your situation to be.
Say: My goals to activate the new story are . . . Practice being open to
finding a solution by focusing the mind on solutions and realizing, *"This
is my drama story,"* in a compassionate, nonjudgmental way that recog-
nizes what is happening so that a shift may follow. *(These are only example
goals in relation to the example story given in this chapter.)*

**Step 6. Invent ways to prevent similar circumstances from trigger-
ing you again.** Pause to look at the *effects* you listed in Step 2 before taking this step, then continue with the following words. I will do damage
control in the future by . . .

Make a list of actions you can take when symptoms from Step 2 express themselves. For example, in the above described situation you
might ask, *"What are the states that I want to feel and actions that I want to take
in place of withdrawal, resentment, and experiencing altered efficiency at work?"*
Name the opposite states, feelings, and actions that you would *prefer* to
experience *and* be sure to write them down:

In the case of the story above, let's say that I decide to name body-
based movement and gratitude practices as my means to focus on
productivity at work when I'm feeling triggered. If so, I would assert
something like the following. *"I now choose to find ways to embody my physical self throughout the day to increase my self-confidence in relation to the space
and people around me. My intention is to heighten my awareness of my physical
self so that I may return to a sense of ease quicker in the event of being triggered.
Strengthening and flexibility movements are to be my focus to also increase my
sense of personal safety and ability to return to a state existing outside of my
trauma drama story."*

After this step, if there is still resentment or negativity, it's a good
idea to focus on gratitude by making mental or paper notes of both
small and large things that you are grateful for. If I was the woman in
the story, if I were to feel new resistance arise to my work (which was
one of the effects of her trauma drama), I would then revisit what I had
logged in my notebook and recite the affirmations that were labeled
Shift Statement and *My Story Reimagined*.

Name That Narrative

Over the next week I want you to designate five or six pages in your journal to the exercise 'Name That Narrative'. Use this technique whenever you hear old or unwanted narrative (aka *non-serving internal dialogue)* as you're going about your day.

Here's how to do it. Observe the words you hear as well as the *tone* of your words. Then, *give a name* to the narrative from the past or recent past that these words most resemble and which you want to transform into supportive, life-enhancing self-talk.

Here is an example: A girl was madly in love with her new partner. She *had* to see him right in that moment. She couldn't wait a day. She was obsessive, sullen, and felt desperate to be with him again. *In her mind.* Because she had read this book and set the intention to practice this exercise, she recognized the voice in her head as intense longing merging with a familiar old desperation. She decided to name this aspect of her current consciousness "The Panic."

Having personified the voice, she started to write about the Panic as if The Panic had already met defeat and had been triumphed over by her own self-awareness.

She writes, *"Dear World,*
You are not going to believe the win I made today! Then again, maybe
you will . . . You know my track record with beating the odds!"

Please notice two things about what she does here. First, she is speaking to the whole world, which is big enough and broad enough to have plenty of people in it who will believe in her *and* her ability to build a new story.

If you, the reader, find this approach helpful, then you may state "Dear World" in your journal like she did. Or if the World is too vast an audience for your taste, try something else. Have you ever seen a tee-shirt that reads "Be the person your dog thinks you are"? Well, that also works. Use any reference or address anyone (or thing) that you wish.

The second component of the girl's message that I'd like you to notice is how she kept her language light and playful. The exercise can be challenging enough if you're trying to overcome habitual patterns—particularly when the topic is as heavy as the state of panic. Allow yourself to explore your dark side with humour whenever you can.

Over the next seven to ten days, write narratives *and* the names you give them to further realize the internal dialogue that plays within you. Go a step further and make a mental note of *how* you have shifted out of the old dialogue and challenged it by building greater awareness around it. Often, the details of the shift are accomplished subconsciously and go unnoticed by the conscious working mind, so it is your job, from the start, to notice *when and how* you first shift out of states such as "The Panic" and therefore you will become more aware of what the catalyst was that has enabled you to victoriously shift.

Here are several globally recurring narrative themes—themes that most people experience periodically. For trauma survivors, they come up more frequently. Be on the lookout for these if you need help to get started.

* **The Worrier**
* **The Over-explainer**
* **The Panic (as mentioned)**
* **The Obsessive**
* **The Self-defeatist**
* **The All Out Cop-Out**
* **The Externally-Focused Competitor**

As you can see from the description above, the Name That Narrative technique is a three-part exercise. Do as much as you can to get started.

For additional resources, free bonuses, one-on-one *and* group coaching opportunities visit www.DiscoverYourResilience.com.

CHAPTER 24

Why Boundaries Are a Gift

❧

BOUNDARIES HELP TO REINFORCE WHAT IS. Boundaries are grounding because they give us a sense of where we are and where other people are within a relationship. Boundaries give us a sense of security and stability when they are spoken responsibly and with a loving presence. Everyone's boundaries are different, however. It is therefore essential to identify what they look like for yourself in order to communicate what your boundaries are in each of your unique and fulfilling relationships.

On the flipside, boundaries get a bad rap at times. I remember when I first learned how to set boundaries. I had announced that I had a physical boundary (which is only one category of boundaries), and the individual I told was looking at me with shock. It seemed that my sharing of my boundary was of dismay to this individual. "Oh, *boundaries . . .* ," the person replied, *"that's ridiculous!"*

It was apparent that this person had an unpleasant experience (or a string of them) around the use of the word *boundaries*. Perhaps this person had been on the receiving end of criticism for "crossing" someone else's boundaries. Later this individual would come around to being compassionate when understanding the logic backing my boundary announcement.

Setting boundaries guarantees us more inner fulfillment and more fulfillment in our relationships. That said, the work of announcing where our boundaries are is not always easy. There are some things we can do to make it an easier, more gratifying action step. At the start and finish line, all we can ever really do in this world is, "Put it out there." Finding a boundary requires self-inquiry and making peace with the truth of what our individual boundaries are. This can really only happen when we accept what they are, *no matter who does or doesn't like them.*

STANDING STRONG

In many people's lives, there is not a convenient or *comfortable* time to share our needs with the people we want in our lives. That's why I call it in an *announcement.*

I realize that for some taking a stand, even with the people whom we adore and appreciate, is akin to the fear that many people have of public speaking. Sometimes speaking our truth can be immobilizing, especially if a particular boundary is rooted in a trauma. When we experience trauma it often creates a new set of circumstances and rules, so to speak, from which we are comfortable to relate our new experience of day-to-day life with people.

The first key to cultivating the type of fulfilling relationships with people who listen and relate is to check in with ourselves as to why we are speaking them in the first place. Are we merely trying to prove a point? Or are we speaking and sharing with the intent of deepening our connection with the person in front of us? We cannot actually *know* meaningful relationship until we relate on terms that are authentic, honest, and genuinely vulnerable.

We know this in our heart of hearts.

It is a fact that for a certain amount of time after trauma life is more challenging. However, I can personally say that the way I relate to people now, although it has not been easy to arrive at this point, is far *more* gratifying to me than the way I related to people was before I experienced a deeply life-changing event.

I am not saying that trauma is a prerequisite to experiencing the depths and fruit of humanity, I am only offering up my experience. I encourage you to take this into consideration in order to assist you, in some way, to bring the effects of your trauma into the light and know that what you experienced is not all bad. *Bad* is a black or white concept, so our relationship with, or our identification with, the word in and of itself can be immobilizing.

Moving forward, let's talk about how we know a boundary has been crossed and then get into the different types of boundaries. I'll give a real-life example of a boundary being crossed.

Several years ago, I began dating someone and we were in the first few months of our relationship. He was very powerful and everything about him was stately. One day, I was at his apartment and didn't know where he'd gone so I called out his name. He said, "I'm over here!" As I started to walk toward his responding voice, I ended up at the doorway of the bathroom where I saw that he was trimming his fingernails while seated on the toilet.

Now, there is nothing wrong with talking to someone while you're on the toilet in many households. However, because we'd been dating for such a short time and because our relationship had a lot of emotional and mental boundaries, many of which were announced to me by him, I was shocked by his invitation to speak with him in this fashion. I always kept the bathroom door shut myself when he was around, so that added to the surprise I felt in this situation. He clearly had assumed that I'd be comfortable with this mode of intimacy. I, on the other hand, was uncertain of what to do or how to respond.

Thankfully, I excused myself from the opening of the doorway where I had caught my first glimpse of my boyfriend and my feet had initially frozen in their tracks.

This is a funny, lighthearted story so we can now effectively look at the principles of identifying boundaries without becoming overwhelmed or getting stuck in the story itself.

Afterward, I requested a forewarning. "Hey," he might have called out, "I'm in the bathroom." There's the forewarning. "I'll be out in a moment!"

Now, given my level of discomfort, what would have happened had I stayed in the doorway? You may guessed correctly, *I would have been crossing my own boundary.*

There is something critical to understand here, which is this. Crossing your own boundaries disrupts the growth and thriving of the self-love that you need in order to take the kind of journey of self-exploration and learning that we're discussing in this book.

How do we know what people's boundaries are? We can ask or they can announce them. Crossing a boundary without knowing it exists doesn't make someone bad, because how can we know we are doing so or others have done so unless those boundaries have been announced?

How can we know when one of our own boundaries has been crossed? My experience shows me that the answer, time and time again, is *from the feeling.* The feeling indicator is essential for growth and change in our relationships. In fact, the more we can be aware of our body-based feelings from moment to moment, the more we can immediately receive notification when we're not comfortable with something or someone else's actions.

Getting in touch with body-based feelings requires development of our curiosity, openness to discovering, acceptance, equilibrium in how we respond (conscious realization combined with self-expression), breathing, and most essentially connection to our bodies. Ways to get in touch with these feelings are numerous, but some ways are more advanced and effective than others. When I name them remember that the quality of these practices also depends on who your guide is, your guide's connection to himself or herself, the guide's connection with the practice mentioned, and essentially the guide's connection with you. Finally, our quality of experience is affected by our willingness to show up and give it our all. Undivided attention in body-based therapies is the key to their success.

Body intelligence is just that—which means it takes time to build and assess. These practices all help build body intelligence. Qigong, tai chi, various forms of yoga, explorative unregimented types of dance (Five

Rhythms®, for example), and progressive Pilates. In addition, gardening, hiking, and walking meditation, in addition to paths of shamanism where the body is encouraged to move in ways that mirror the natural rhythms of life are fantastic as well.

BOUNDARY-SETTING EXERCISE
Remember, knowledge is not power. Knowledge *applied* is power. Therefore, I invite you to do a boundary-setting exercise right now. Choose one individual with whom you have a key relationship. Ensure that this is someone you've been relating with for at least six months so that you'll have enough experiences to reflect upon. You may choose a friend, a romantic partner, a spouse, a family member, a coworker, a neighbour, a boss, or an employee as your subject. You'll need paper and pen.

On the left side of your paper, write the following words in a vertical column just like you see here. List these precise words.

* Mental
* Emotional
* Physical
* Energetic
* Transient
* Permanent
* Spoken
* Unspoken
* Realized
* Unrealized

STEP 1: IDENTIFY IF YOU HAVE ANNOUNCED A BOUNDARY
The first step is to go through each of the categories of boundaries on your list with your chosen person in mind, and write *yes* or *not yet* beside each.

First, can you think of a *mental boundary* that you ever announced to this person? For example, a mental boundary I announced to my partner was not to talk about previous relationships he's had. So I put yes next to *mental boundary*.

Remember, whatever your subject's reaction was when you announced a particular boundary doesn't matter for this step, as it is strictly your boundaries that you are evaluating for now.

After finding a mental boundary you've announced, you'll do the same thing with the listing of an emotional boundary that you've announced with the person you have chosen to keep in mind. This is only if applicable, of course. If you have not spoken one or more of these types of boundaries then simply write *not yet* beside it.

Here are exact definitions of each of the types of boundaries . . .

Mental boundaries are things, people, or places that you do not want to discuss with other people for the time being. These are subjects that you are aware have an unhealthy effect on your well-being so you choose *not* to discuss them whether temporarily or permanently.

Emotional boundaries are boundaries set up around either your expression or someone else's open expression of an emotion. It may just so happen that you personally are uncomfortable with being around certain expressions of anger, even if it is a safe method with the intent of discharging the anger, such as pounding a pillow. You may have announced to a friend who asked permission to do this in your presence, "*No way!* Anger scares the *bee-gee-gees* out of me! And even the *responsible* expression of it triggers *way too much* anxiety for me to be in the same room—or even the same building, for that matter! So I'd rather you just tell me that we have to continue our hang out another day so I am *not* present for that."

If you have made an announcement like this, then you may mark the emotional category with *yes*. And perhaps one or two words to jog your memory listed beside that *yes* so you can easily recollect the last time you spoke an emotional boundary.

Having an emotional boundary also translates as you willingly feeling as you feel in a moment without being swayed from feeling that feeling.

It can be the announcement that you have "the right" to feel something that you are feeling even if no one else is feeling it at the same time you are. Ultimately, it may be that you are requesting to be a compassionate witness for a friend or loved one who is experiencing whatever emotion they are having although you cannot, for whatever reason, share in it. It is essentially the announcement that you are honoring whatever it is that you are feeling, or whatever it is that they are feeling, *without expecting yourself or them to be on the exact same page.*

An example of crossing an emotional boundary is if someone is trying to control, discount, stop, or suggest and/or influence what another person's emotional state "should" be.

As you saw above, there are ten categories of boundary. I'd like to continue giving you definitions of the remaining eight types, so that you'll know whether to say *yes* or *not yet*.

Physical boundaries are points of contact that you do not feel comfortable with if they are enacted by another. For example, I when I taught yoga in Vancouver, Canada, I would ask who did or didn't want an assisted-stretch of the Achilles heel at the end of class. Also, my students had the opportunity to raise their hands when we participated in the life exploration, interactive, spoken part of class. Had they walked up to the front of the room and waved a hand in my face I would have announced that they were crossing a physical boundary.

Energetic boundaries relate to the energetic selves that expand beyond our physical selves. At the very least the energy body takes up the space that is arm's length in every direction as far as we can reach. Some refer to this space as the aura, or playfully as an *energetic space-ship* because it contains your physical self and at the same time when tapped into can take you to new places within yourself. Scientifically, it is known as the *electromagnetic field* (EMF). This is both strengthened and weakened by various emotional, mental, and physical factors within our environments.

Here is an example of an energetic boundary, let's say that no one is directly touching you or saying anything to you, but you are sharing a live, work, or play space with a person. This individual is sitting ten feet away from you and every time that his phone vibrate he does a little whistle and excitedly jumps a little in his seat, before saying, *"Yes!"*

Now, the person is not doing anything directly *to you*, in fact he's not even interacting with you. . . but he is, without even meaning to, affecting your energetic well-being as you are currently intending to be in a self-induced calm and serene state. The space you are sharing is being affected partially by their action and partially by your response to it.

So, what to do?

First of all, you may or may not choose to mention anything because you may or may not know this person. The announcement in this situation may be *to yourself.* You are simply admitting that the disturbance is having an internal impact on you and then deciding what you will do about it from a place of self-love. Will you get up and leave? Or move to another table, desk, or spot in the room?

If you can recollect a time when you addressed a situation like this *write it down!*

Fortunately, you don't need to think about what other people are thinking about you as you participate in this exercise. *Besides, that's brain robbery* and it's up to you whether or not you're going to let your thoughts and mental space be hijacked!

Transient boundaries are time-contingent, time-sensitive boundaries comprised of either mental, emotional, physical or energetic components. For example, if you have had surgery and the doctor says, "No physical activity. Rest only." Then, you are working with a transient, temporary boundary.

Or if you're studying hard for a job promotion and cannot see a dear friend for that whole week then you announce that you have a temporary boundary and cannot see them or speak with them as much for those seven days. There are transient emotional boundaries, transient physical boundaries, transient mental boundaries, and transient energetic boundaries. A denying of a transient energetic boundary is if you were to have a friend who calls you three times a day or texts three times a day just to say hi even though you told them that you are unavailable to talk (mental boundary) or hang out (physical boundary) for the seven days. You can feel them wanting your attention, yet they indeed are not breaching any other boundaries (physical, emotional, or mental).

Communicating transient boundaries can help relationships stay in harmony because they provide a sense of security when people know and understand the length and extent of your intended boundaries.

Permanent boundaries are the boundaries that are *not* flexible to change for whatever personal or public reason that we may have. The reason for permanent boundaries being a necessary staple in our lives, supporting our greatest good, is because they reflect and preserve the core values found within our individual center. A permanent boundary may be not to go clubbing because it lessens authentic interaction and communication. Or it may be the decision to stay away from the neighborhood where your abusive parent raised you because of the pain and old memories that visiting that area stirs up because one of your core values may be to feel *as much joy in your life as possible.*

Spoken boundaries are boundaries made known. Spoken boundaries are when all parties involved are made aware of the boundary. Spoken boundaries are an opportunity to make amends with the person or people involved. They are the necessary communication of what is most true to the individual(s) who speaks them. They may be new to the person/people speaking them or they may be boundaries that have been alive and well within the individual that have not been known in the past to others for whatever reason.

Unspoken boundaries are boundaries known by an individual only. It is often assumed by that same person that everyone else knows them. However, unspoken boundaries can sometimes be unknown to the person who has a boundary, but has not yet consciously come to know that she has a boundary which is a key to her ultimate well-being. Unspoken boundaries are more common than we may realize, as we as people learn by trial and error. Thus, we learn by experience. Sometimes an experience will tip us off that we have a boundary in a place or facet of our lives and existence that has gone unrealized by us and thus neglected *by us* up until this point.

After all, it is not always a sure thing that someone will know another's boundary unless it is spoken or a person is highly intuitive.

In this case, for this exercise, I welcome you to consider a time when you were surprised that someone didn't know you had a boundary that *you assumed* he or she knew you had. Or vice versa, contemplate a time that someone was surprised that you didn't know he or she had a specific boundary. Also remember to think about *what you want different* regarding actions, thoughts, and patterns that you take versus listing what you want someone else to change when you come to that part of the exercise noted as Step 3.

Realized boundaries are simply boundaries that you have a high awareness that you have or someone else has.

Unrealized boundaries are a main source of conflict and misunderstanding. When someone has a deep-seated boundary, but is not consciously aware of it, it is an unrealized boundary. In this case, what is not known cannot be responsibly communicated.

Think about the different categories of your life and consider how satisfied you are with them: home, work, family, boyfriend/girlfriend, colleagues, sport, recreation, social . . .

Is there perhaps an unrealized boundary that you want to announce, but haven't? If yes, I invite you to write it down!

Let us remember that in a healthy relationship *spoken, realized* boundaries do not drive wedges between us and others. They promote greater connection and strength of the bond.

STEP 2: RATE YOUR SATISFACTION

After you've identified whether or not you've announced the mentioned types of boundaries above to past or present people in your lives, go back through the list one more time to rate how satisfied you are with the current state of the boundary.

Rate them from 1–3.

1 = Not satisfied
2 = Somewhat satisfied
3 = Very satisfied.

This is where you'll be able to indicate if someone has crossed one of your boundaries or respected it and vice versa. It's also an opportunity to notice if you constantly cross your own boundaries by remaining in relationships to the same level of commitment as previously, even if someone has not listened to your spoken boundary request.

STEP THREE: NAME SOMETHING YOU WANT TO CHANGE
For the categories of boundaries that you rated only a 1 or 2, mention one thing that you want to change. It can be anything. Allow yourself to dream a little when focusing on this step (or dream a lot). Come up with a specific change for each category on your paper.

STEP FOUR: NAME THE FEELING YOU DESIRE TO FEEL
Now, come up with one feeling word that describes your state of being after the one thing in each boundary category has changed. You honestly won't know the power of this step until you do it. It's empowering.

For example, a student of mine in Vancouver, Canada, had always been called Sue by her mother although she had always asked her mother to call her by her full name, Suzanne. Her mother claimed that she never wanted her name to be Suzanne in the first place, but that her father had chosen the name. For whatever rightful reason, Suzanne never liked the named Sue. It made her feel "cutesy" and "little girlish," "understated," "unseen," and "unhonored." At age ten or so, Suzanne stopped asking her mom to call her by her full name. She gave up in realization that she couldn't change her mom. As an adult it was still a realized *though unspoken* boundary.

Suzanne's mother was shocked when she brought it up again and laughed saying now that her daughter was an adult she surely didn't mind calling her whatever she wanted to be called. Suzanne had realized the impact of being called Sue by doing this exercise when she got to figuring out how happy she was or wasn't with her family's unspoken boundaries. Now twenty-six, she could see that she herself had given up on her dream to be called by her full name because when she imagined how she would feel if her name was honored she felt a lightness that she hadn't felt in a long time in life in general. In just imagining that her mom listened to her request, she felt a deep sense of gratitude toward her mother that had always been foreign to her previously.

CHAPTER 25

How to Break Through Denial

❦

Breaking through denial is a very important thing to do after trauma because when you couple denial with trauma it can lead you down a path of discontentment with everything around you. Denial is a trap because it takes a lot of energy to pretend something didn't happen or isn't the way it is. What you might not have realized yet is that everything around you might be different and improving for the best, if so much of your energy weren't being invested in focusing on your pre-trauma climate. The truth is that life is challenging enough without the additional burden of pretending that one of your biggest life experiences hasn't occurred. Trauma has its own blessings waiting to be revealed. By accepting the traumatic experience has happened there are rich insights about self *and life* to follow that will only build an even more magnificent life experience for you.

Denial can cause the body to fall into a state of disrepair and disease. I know this firsthand. Instead of talking to a counselor or psychologist about the challenges I faced during the eight years of being one of my dad's main caretakers and how it was for me, during my youth, as I more often than not worried about leaving the house for fear he would be dead when I came back—or discussing the impact of his ultimate death on me—I looked to food to solve everything for me. I used food to help me numb the emotions I was unwilling to feel.

By the time my father died, when I was sixteen, I was in the mode of thinking I needed to control everything. I denied my experience of grief and my relief. As a result of my denial, I started controlling my body. In only a year, I went from being overweight, eating fast food regularly, and drinking alcohol to spending five days at the gym and walking at the beach on Sunday, and eating only pure whole foods in the form of apples and nonfat pan spray-cooked spinach. Although this may sound good, my measure of success was if I didn't eat any fat *at all!* My body was starving for the GOOD fats found in avocados and buttered potatoes! Everything had to be steamed or boiled. On the weekends, when I drank at friends' houses I would gauge myself in a drunken state to make up for the lack of fat the other five days a week. Thankfully, I wasn't bulimic at any point during this phase. Even so, I recognize now that not eating any fat is OBSESSIVE and LIFE LIMITING! Try to go to a social event or friend's house and NOT eat fat. It's ridiculously hard on you, and also self-centered to place so many food requests on the cook of the evening.

Denial of trauma can look like being seventeen in New York City and experiencing rape and not admitting it happened, which is what I did because of my pride and fear of what others, in particular my mother, would say have to about it. In addition to the great deal of shame I felt for having had the boundaries of my body disrespected and violated, I was in a deep state of denial for several months. My body responded by nearly shutting down. I drank so heavily to numb out my feelings one day that I wound up in a Manhattan hospital without any friends or emotional support with me. I had gotten to the hospital in a stretcher, after calling 9-1-1 myself. Then I was immobilized for two days and throwing up the contents of my stomach—a bright, neon green mess.

To the body there is no such thing as denial. We can try to lie to ourselves by doing things to trick our minds, but we can never lie to our bodies. What we're not facing will catch up to us. It will express itself through signs that can be read in the body.

Thankfully, a year after landing in that hospital in New York I found myself standing on a yoga mat—my first. Four years after that, I was teaching my first yoga class after completing a 500-hour intensive yoga teacher training program in Canada. Denial, by then, had turned into listening to, surrendering to, *accepting*, and *loving* my body and *everything it has to tell me.*

    (Long live healthy fats!)

Develop Your Feeling Detector

ॐ

IF I WERE TO TELL YOU that I intentionally go from feeling sadness to feeling joy in just under five minutes what would you think? What if I told you that doing so is a system that the evolution of human biology created in order to prevent us from sinking into any one feeling state for too long?

You may wonder what the danger of being in any one emotional state for too long is . . . The answer to that is, in fact, subjective, mostly because of the fact that in our culture emotions are rarely talked about in a productive sense and rarely brought to our undivided, *nonjudgmental* attention. You may also be wondering what this system is. After all, aren't we feeling and emotional beings by the grace of God and by the design of our biological makeup?

The point here, to begin this chapter, is that when our feelings are engaged consciously, it takes the experience of beingness to a whole new level.

Making an unbiased, innocent inquiry into where we are within our emotional selves throughout the day is exactly what needs to happen in order for us to master our emotions and end the trauma drama in our lives. What we hold onto, we become. What we honor through observation, we liberate from being our sole reality. Feelings are powerful, ignore them and they will rule you.

Many people feel too ashamed of their emotions to discuss them, especially boys and men, as is documented in the film *The Mask You Live*

In. However, treating emotions as a danger to be avoided only amasses more of the very emotion one is *trying* to push away. Changing our feeling experience is accomplished by changing our thought experience, which is a good thing to do, but only after first *evaluating our feelings,* which takes practice, acceptance, and most of all *willingness.*

Last summer, as I drove through the farmland outside of Vancouver, British Columbia, I listened to motivational speaker Les Brown talk about his vast life experiences. I noticed how he is capable of shifting from one vibrational frequency, or *feeling experience*, to another relatively quickly. Perhaps it was my appreciation for the speaker that put my subconscious mind to work. What I wrote down that day while pausing at stop signs and traffic lights was the following string of words:

* Sadness
* Anger
* Hopefulness
* Satisfaction
* Desire
* Purposefulness
* Happiness
* Pleasure
* Joy

That day, through conscious self-encouraged reflection, I discovered the order of experience of my feeling states. I learned that by choosing to evaluate the unique ordering of my feeling experiences—by becoming aware of what they are, and taking the time to write them down to remember them—we are taking the first step in tapping into a powerful tool to shift from being stuck in any one particular state of being. If you can guess *or know* which emotional frequency will follow the one you are currently experiencing, especially when in a tough spot, you are elevating your life experience by giving yourself the freedom not to become over-identified with one state--especially when it doesn't serve you.

It is important to emphasize that the path to the mastery of our emotions is not about changing the feelings we have or the emotions we express, but rather about the purity of accepting them. By embracing our emotions rather than pushing them away, we can begin to live as energetically free and clear as we did when we were children.

As Aristotle says, "Excellence is a habit." By developing the habit of patterning our emotions, we can work through them more succinctly and effectively when they come up at the random times that they do. We can ignite a sense of ownership of our experience and by doing so lessen blame and confusion, as well as reduce the length of our bouts of hurt, rage and depression.

This is what I propose you do. Imagine a time in your life that was unpleasant or sad. Then, feel into your body to become familiar with what the sensations are *or* where your body lacks sensation. Put your focused attention on your breath as a grounding tool. Begin to sense what physical sensations, feelings, and emotions habitually come directly *after* the state of the self-suggested state of sadness or unpleasantness, depending on which one you have chosen to begin this exercise. From there, continue to inquire into what the feeling evolves into next after you have observed and stayed with the physical sensations that arose. We are exercising the muscle of awareness here by choosing *not* to *attach* to it or *ignore* it. Instead *tune* into the feelings one-by-one like you would a radio program that you are neither excited about nor indifferent to. You have a healthy level of interest. No ignoring. No attaching.

My own progression of feelings typically move me from sadness to anger to hopefulness to satisfaction.

In what order is your unique progression?

Beginning with the more challenging internal experiences, such as sadness or disappointment, observe where you go next. If and when you choose to practice this exercise, it is best to start with the feeling that you struggle with most. Pause for a moment and think of what that is. For me, at the time in my life when I discovered this technique, it was sadness and a feeling of loss. So I quietly asked myself what sadness felt like in my body. It was a feeling of heaviness in my legs. As I focused on the sense of heaviness in my lower body *without wanting to change it and with curiosity as an introduced secondary component,* I noticed that there was anger accompanied with the feeling of restriction in my chest. My experience continued to evolve as I tapped into my full experience as you may read within the bulleted list above.

By beginning to acknowledge physical associations that link to the list of feelings that you come up with, you can draw upon what it means to master your emotional self by learning *when* you want to shift and *what* you want to shift to next.

Remember, the process of emotional mastery is not about changing how you feel; it's about completely embracing each state of being in order to shift onto the next without becoming victim to one that's a disservice to you as a whole being. When our emotional self is healthy each state of being naturally transcends and shifts into the next realized feeling. Observe children's healthy transition from one state to another: there is little to no resistance and the child is often receptive to suggestions to move on from what is currently taking place. If the children you know in your life are not so agreeable, then consider when you were a child: did you get stuck in any one place for too long? No, of course not. Because you were too busy being receptive to life and what it was offering next!

ADDING IMAGERY

For me, I learned that the thought of leaping into the middle of a pile of fall leaves creates a sense of joy because of the childhood memories I have associated with doing so. That gives me an image I can return to when I want to restore my feelings of joy quickly. When I think of sad, I think of imagery that isn't too overwhelming, as I suggest you also follow this suggestion. For instance, I think of being away on a trip and how much I miss my dog and how I feel sad everytime I see someone who is out walking their dog. The introduction of imagery is best to begin with baby steps. When we start small we build confidence and we remedy the possibility of becoming overwhelmed with this portion of the exercise.

What's it All About?

The purpose of this exercise is to become more *familiar* with your ability to shift quickly from potentially limiting states of feeling experience to productive ones. Through practicing our emotions, we develop our ability to focus, and this ensures that we will not have unwanted stagnation in our lives.

As you navigate through and learn about your unique emotional patterns and tendencies, by anchoring yourself in your body sensations you will begin to experience true *aliveness*. Even the sounds, words, and sights that come to mind when focusing on each feeling experience can help to anchor you if you wish to integrate these into your exploration. As you increasingly sense and remain connected to your inner self, a great store of life energy will be brought to you.

You will need this life energy that *responding* to your feelings gives you versus *reacting* to your feelings which in turn depletes you.

Engaging Yourself

As I was winding down from writing this piece, I took a walk in the rainforest near my house. I ran into a woman who was on route to a Pilates class. She was enthusiastic about expressing the benefits of intentional body movement. I couldn't help but notice the correlation between intending to connect with the body when in movement and the marked differences it produces for the whole self and the vast benefits described above that are produced when we intentionally come into contact with our emotional selves.

We talked about the effectiveness of focused, intentional movement versus the types of sporadic, unpracticed, and disengaged movements that come from doing things such as taking a walk while making a grocery list in your mind or riding a stationary bike while talking on the phone. I immediately thought about the difference between allowing ourselves to ride around on the unpredictable and oftentimes unruly wave of emotions versus intentionally tuning into the internal responses to our environments throughout the day and giving them the attention they deserve. Without becoming attached. Without ignoring them to the demise of the rest of our being.

The more focus and *thus involvement* we give to the moment, when we're physically moving, the more mental, emotional and physical toxins that we burn. The more *aware* we become of our emotions the more physically and mentally comfortable we become throughout the day. All components of ourselves are interconnected: body, mind, feelings and spirit. As we give each one the attention they deserve the healthier we become as a whole.

I suggest that the same goes for mind-based exercises: The more focused, intentional and purposeful our thoughts are in the moment, the more *realized* and *unrealized* anxiety we burn off from our emotional selves and the more resistance to change we counteract.

LET'S FACE IT

It takes energy to put effort into our lives and the thoughts we choose. It takes *energy* to carefully create and believe *in our thoughts.* Therefore, to choose and select our emotional vibration, once we have honored where we are by first sitting with our present feeling and recognizing it for what it is, either with a friend or in your journal with the above consciousness exercise, we more easily burn off mental and physical stress and inertia. As a result, we have more energy for our day-to-day activities and the unknown. Honoring our feelings through recognition feeds energy to our minds and to our bodies. The more we do so the more this is true!

It's Your Turn Now

Get a piece of paper out and pen or pencil. Either carry these around with you throughout the day or do this exercise at the end of the day to reflect on the day's experiences. Write down each of your day's most meaningful experiences, *including one feeling word for each experience.*

Now, write down one reason at minimum that you are grateful for each experience. Begin a gratitude sentence like this: "I am grateful for the experience even though it was challenging and I felt _____ (fill in the blank with a feeling word, such as *frustrated)* because I learned _____ (fill in the blank with a discovery) about myself."

Follow up by speaking this affirmation, "I am grateful for my strength and my resilience. I embrace the greatness of my *whole* self, *feelings and all.*"

This exercise gives us the opportunity to continue to create *and embrace* rich and rewarding life experiences. The ability to do so is a key healer after the experience of trauma.

Honoring What is

It is possible for us to *use* our senses to bring us back into the moment, even though as modern-day humans we've been taught to use our senses to distract us from what we are feeling deep down. For example, if we feel nervous, instead of eating junk food to blanket the feeling of nervousness, we can realize a way to *tap into* that nervousness *and use it for our gain.* Let's say that when we are restless, instead of turning on the television we walk around the block to transform the restlessness into cultivated fearlessness and personal power. We then apply that strengthened sense of self to the areas of our lives that need it.

We may not be able to change areas of our lives right away, but we can build into what we can change and influence, and we will see the effects in the areas where we were previously struggling. And all because we focused in on how we are feeling in any given moment, without judgment and without the desire to ignore or distract from that feeling.

Negative states of feeling and being are transient *and* multifaceted. All feelings morph into another embodiment of being, and with awareness and intention this happens even more quickly.

GOING DEEPER: QUESTION YOUR ASSUMPTIONS

Sometimes I am . . . no . . . I *feel* sad. To identify with the word *sad* is to identify with someone else's concept. Sad is a concept, after all. In fact, there are many kinds of sadness.

Does everyone have words for the different kinds of sadness? No. So, people tag one word onto an assortment of feelings.

Why? Because it's easier. Once you put a label on something you automatically stop thinking about it. You succumb to "being" the word sad or "being" angry, and so forth without investigating further why, or what it's all about.

To tag a feeling before you take the time to sense its natural complexity is to resultingly over-identify with a largely unexplored concept. And it is to sit latent in that word and all of the mainstream understanding about the word.

We must intend to *explore* what every feeling is rather than sitting complacently in our feelings. This is empowerment. To listen to ourselves. And, to learn from ourselves . . . in order to transform ourselves.

CHAPTER 27

Practice Moderation

❧

THIS APPLIES TO EVERYTHING IN life. During coaching school, I had a teacher with whom I resonated deeply, so we maintained a friendship afterward. Little did I know that his real teaching of me would come into effect after my course had ended. By watching how this individual lived, I made some discoveries. Despite his knowledge as a coach and his excellence as a teacher, I saw that he gave so much of his time and energy away that he wasn't saving anything for himself. His personal life reflected this lack in everything from eating an improper diet, to poor health, and a deprivation of relationships.

He was trying to save other people to his own detriment.

Shortly after, on Facebook, I saw a random post in my newsfeed that read something to the effect of, *"Work Smarter, Not Martyr!"*

Seeing my friend struggling, I realized that I needed always to come from a place of balance in my life in order to be truly of service both to myself and to the people I have signed up to serve. Since then I have aimed to give in moderation rather than excessively, including moderation in everything I do. This has led me to decisions to take more walks, spend time with furry friends, and stop working past a certain hour each day.

I do not have a glossy idea of what moderation looks like for you. I do know that it is a part of our *experience* when we balance our actions and behaviors to consider *both* ourselves and other people. In this case we are not looking for the kind of balance that enables us to stand on one leg while in the grocery checkout line (although if you're in need of physical fitness that could be a great way to balance your family obligations with fun and health)! I also do not mean that balance magically appears when we introduce all the parts of life into our lifestyles that society tells us we should partake in. If you're not a gym goer or a marathon runner then those are realistically not part of the formula that brings moderation to *your* life.

We have discovered the ability to strike an inner sense of balance *when we have the energy to do all the things that we most love to do.* Knowing whether or not we have enough energy to do the things that bring the most happiness to our lives is something only we can tell ourselves. No one else can *feel* that for us other than ourselves.

Furthermore, it does not matter how much or how little we work, but rather that we have a sense of passion and enthusiasm in what we do when we show up.

In the cultivation of moderation, I am talking about the meeting of an authentic self that is centered in well-being, which is our own personal definition of balance *based on how we feel.* That is the ultimate goal when it comes to being able to stabilize your life and succeed and *thrive* after trauma. We must give ourselves back what was taken from us by the experience of abandoning *how we felt,* in order to protect ourselves in that past moment of trauma, abuse, or violence.

We can only do this if we are honest about how we feel in each breathing moment.

The bottom line is that when you seek moderation do not go by the *shoulds.* Do not go by what every magazine article or highway billboard has told you about balance.

CHAPTER 28

Do This Exercise!

❧

YOU'LL BEGIN TO HEIGHTEN YOUR self-awareness if you do this exercise once a day at the end of the day. You may always do it more often, if you like.

For this exercise, you'll need pen and paper. Draw a vertical line, creating two columns on the paper. Then label one column with "What" at the top and the other with "Why" at the top, so that these headlines are side by side and separated only by the line you drew. The left column represents what you did today and the right column explains why you did it.

Write down as many actions as you took and then assess your motivations.

Set aside judgment when you do this exercise. You don't need to do anything else other than write in these two columns to build greater awareness throughout your days. This simple yet routinely powerful exercise also serves to engage and therefore balance both the left and right hemispheres of the brain. It puts them in communication with one another. Whereas, it is possible that traumatic experiences may create a disconnect between the two. This exercise is to empower you and your general life awareness.

The Best Question for Helpers to Ask

ॐ

WHAT'S THE BEST QUESTION YOU can ask someone who has experienced a trauma (regardless of when it occurred) in order to assist their optimal healing?

The answer is: "How are you *now?*"

The best way to console someone who has experienced a traumatic experience is to be present for them. Nothing more, *nothing less.* People who've been through something painful need this more than advice, more than sympathy, and more than being left alone "for the sake of their privacy."

If you're in the least uncomfortable because you've never experienced what they've experienced, you can create a sense of safety for yourself when making yourself available to listen by setting a time boundary. Say, as you look down at your watch or phone, "I have five minutes, do you want to catch up? I'd love to hear how you're doing." Then, it's important that you simply listen, no matter what they say. Really give your heart's ear to what is being said to you.

Remember, that no matter where they are, no matter how emotional or messed up they seem to you, expressing it is a phase of their healing experience. So do not detract from their experience or shift the focus from them by reacting wildly. Saying, *"Oh, that's so horrible!"* locks them into the state they're in or trying to cheerlead them on and make them feel better may cause them to become insecure with where they are in their healing and what they really are feeling. You run the risk of making them feel foolish for feeling awful and not "being fixed" quickly enough.

As friends and family, healers, coaches, and counselors, we do not want people to do the work of healing their pain and the great myriad of effects of their trauma for the sake of our praise. We want them to improve for themselves. That's what creates lasting change.

At the end of the day, people want to be witnessed. That's all. Some people may say they want your advice as a friend, parent, sister, friend, or therapist, but what they're really saying is, "I want to connect." When we're feeling traumatized, we want to connect with someone who isn't scared of the experience we've been through, as well as with someone who doesn't fear the truth that any number of unexpected occurrences can occur within each of our lives while we are living on this planet.

It takes courage to both acknowledge that and be okay with that.

It is an absolute that the unknown is part of our earthly existence. And I can assure you that nothing is scarier and more dispiriting than fearing an experience that one of our loved ones has encountered. It leaves us feeling like cowards and useless to console the ones we care about deeply. For this reason, we must learn how to come face on with the hurt of our loved ones and ourselves. Otherwise, we run from it and create additional dramas where there previously weren't any.

Nothing is more empowering than standing up to the unknown, becoming curious, and being present for those who we care about. Whatever our loved ones are going through is a phase and a phase we have no control over. By offering a few, uninterrupted moments of your time to those that have experienced something especially traumatic, you are advocating for their healing. Whether or not you know it!

This is important to them because it is possible that they are not yet able to stand up or advocate for themselves. Maybe no one has heard them before. Or maybe people have tried to listen, and have even offered to listen at intentional, set times, but haven't been ready to truly listen yet.

If your loved one, friend, or client is not ready to talk yet be patient and try again later. Recovery happens in its own time. Healing, by its own nature, is not to be forced. It is an organic process.

Healing the *story* of the trauma is an exceptionally important aspect of trauma recovery. Trauma has the tendency to flood our current perception of the moment because it takes time to process and heal all the details of the trauma. When and if a person is lost in the story of an event, being present to where they are in the story *now* will help them to build clarity.

It sounds simple, right? It's not. But *it is possible.*

In today's fast-paced world making sense of pain and getting clarity about what we have experienced is the ultimate blessing.

Will you put your phone in airplane mode, your computer on hibernate, your iPod on pause for five minutes to demonstrate your commitment to your friend or loved one or yourself this week?

CHAPTER 30

What's in a Yes *for You?*

∽

IT'S IMPORTANT TO KNOW THE answer to this when you practice your affirmations. What's a yes?

What does your head do when you say yes?

What does your mouth do after you said yes to something very exciting, like a special and exciting proposed idea from a friend, colleague, or loved one?

What do you notice happens energetically when you are saying yes? What about right after you say yes? Imagine for a moment that someone says they're going to take care of your kids for a week so that you can go on a vacation. Or imagine that someone's giving you $50,000 for your startup business and they ask you, "Do you want this?" And then, in both cases, that you exclaim, "Yes!" How does your energy move in your body and around your body after you say yes wholeheartedly to something wonderful in your life?

You can find an answer to this question if you focus on the area just off your skin. Lie in a supine position where you can be restful and observant of your state of mind and your body. Focus then on the area just off of your skin as you answer the above questions. What shifts for you when you say yes, as you are imagining these special circumstances, right in the area off of the skin? Do you feel more space around you? Do you feel more expansive physically as if you are OK to take up more space?

Saying words is one thing. Actually feeling and energizing the words with your mind body and energetic self is the necessary addition in order to shift our felt, and thus lived, realities.

Explore what yes is to your body and whole being by writing down what you notice as you imagine circumstances that are pleasing. They can be situations that have presented themselves in your experience as of the last year OR they can be situations that you WANT to happen and are willing to explore how they feel in your body as you: 1) hold the picture in your mind of them happening, and 2) nod your head while smiling and essentially saying yes in your whole body and focused mind.

Now, write down what the yes feels like in your body-mind complex. Maybe it feels like a sentence such as, "I can do anything!" Or, maybe it feels like a big grin and butterflies in your stomach. Find out what YES means to you: your body, your mind, your spirit, and your emotional self!

CHAPTER 31

What Do You Do When
the *Universe* Says Yes?

෴

WHEN THE UNIVERSE IS SAYING yes, **KEEP GOING!** Continue making strides and make requests of the world, God, and the universe. Whether you ask of the world first or ask God first matters, in my opinion. Do not ask anything of the world and its citizens until you ask the universe or The Creator for confirmation that whatever it is has a rightful place in your life at this place and time.

When we ask for something we want with the full purity found within the heart, the felt presence of the universe often seems to be running through us from our fingertips to our toes. The universe is full of energy and the best place to begin to secure that energy is in our present being. Therefore, before you go to anyone for anything, build up the God-given field of energy around you.

Does this sound like hocus pocus? It's not. Anybody who logs into Google, picks up a book on physics, or enrolls in a science class can learn how the body emits an electromagnetic field. This bioelectrical field is strengthened and weakened by different components of our environment. The body's energy field can be strengthened by the presence of other living things that also possess a nature-generated magnetic field, including animals and plants.

If you're ever feeling drained, go to these elements of the natural world for renewal. Simply touching a tree or an animal (both are a reflection and part of God) or even sitting close to them will strengthen your energy field which in turn will strengthen your body. When we feel physically strong we feel strong in mind and spirit, too. Use this to your advantage. Awareness is key. And, make sure to take a moment to give silent or aloud gratitude for all that God has created naturally.

It is worthwhile to note that whereas nature-generated fields strengthen our energy, machine-generated fields weaken the energy body. Although I am not a scientist, the amount of time that I have spent exploring the power of bioelectrical fields over the last several years and listening to what doctors from universities like Karolinska Institute in Oslo, Sweden, to Harvard University in Cambridge, Massachusetts, in the United States have to say about the subject, I am certain that we can improve our ability to succeed after trauma through the help of harnessing our positive personal power accessible by building our own personal electromagnetic field.

The exercises and considerations found in this book help you to fully merge the power of your mind, your intention, and your own energy to gradually conquer trauma drama one day at a time.

PART THREE

Create Your Life Now
Techniques for Triumph

❧

CHAPTER 32

How to Embrace Your Body's Experience

❧

IN THIS CHAPTER, WE WILL visit a few tips on how to dialogue with our bodies in order to redesign our relationship with them and heal the physical remnants of our trauma. In the following exercise, we learn how to *listen to our bodies* and *speak to our bodies*. When I created this exercise I was inspired by the previous work of Babette Rothschild and Louise Hay.

THE BODY AS STORY EXERCISE

You'll want a piece of paper and a pen to do this process. The Body as Story process begins with simple inquiry. Ask: *"What do I feel right now?"*

Listen to your body. Then, write down the answer.

If you felt an ailment, tension, pain, or any kind of bodily discomfort, then once you have the detailed answer to your question, the next step is to troubleshoot it.

Ask: *"What experience do I want my body to have?*

Sit quietly and breathe into any sense of discomfort you may feel. Speak the following mantra as many times in a row as needed in order to shift into a receptive and open state of being.

"The world is a friendly place for me to live, breathe, and prosper."

183

Once you feel open to changing your felt experience in this exercise, then create, write, and say the mantra you've chosen for yourself, either silently or aloud, while maintaining focused connection with your breath. This single-pointed focus of concentrating on your self-appointed mantra, while staying present with your breath and thus physical experience, is your meditation for the moment. Treat it as such and give your full presence to the words.

After you've repeated your self-given mantra, write down what you *now* feel in your body. Focus your mind on interpreting the *life-giving* feelings you have rather than on any restrictive or painful feelings that may be there. In other words, focus on the light at the end of the tunnel. Then ask yourself: *"What subtle shifts do I feel?"*

If you can't peg your feeling in words, sit quietly and observe the shift in your body for a few minutes. Sense the vibration of the shifted energy in your body. See if you can notice how from moment to moment the body vibrates at different levels of felt energy.

Research shows that the body is affected by words and thoughts, so pay equal attention to the *intention* you're putting into your words at this point. Be open to the idea of raising your vibration with your selected high-energy, positive-minded, mantra.

Now that you've connected physically, mentally, and intuitively with your body, you are that much more capable to integrate these three elements of who you are. I recommend that you do a basic yoga pose to strengthen the connection between your body, mind, and spirit. For the last part of this exercise, either choose a yoga movement that you know how to do and feel best mirrors how you now feel internally after meditating on your mantra, *or* if you do not know how to practice any yoga postures at this time utilise the free yoga instruction videos found online at SteadyStreamWellness.com.

As you're choosing the best yoga pose to accompany the words of an affirmative mantra, do your best to listen to *how you energetically feel* and connect this with your chosen physical expression. The physical movement or pose you choose is meant to be your opportunity to demonstrate your renewed and deepened connection with your vibrant whole self. Remember to choose one that you feel will help you fully embody the words of your chosen mantra.

For example, if your mantra is "I stand in strength and full knowing that I am deserving of a great life," then the pose you do may be as simple as standing in Mountain Pose. This is with your big toes touching and heels slightly apart, your shoulder blades dropping down your back, your chest softened (though rising upward), and your palms spreading out and facing forward to invigorate the energetic of forward motion, receptivity and progress.

Here's another example. If your mantra today is "I trust in my courage to bring me to the places I am meant to be," then practicing Eagle Pose might be more fitting for you.

For added effectiveness, next print out a photo of yourself embodying the pose and glue or tape it to a piece of construction paper or a whiteboard with your specific life-affirming sentence. Write the mantra related to the photo directly beneath it in big, legible letters.

Continue making life-affirming posters like this one until you have posters of ten full poses along with their connected life-affirming thoughts. Be sure to bring out one of the posters you've created so you can see it in plain view every morning while still in comfortable clothes. As you stand before it, bring your chin parallel to the floor. Lift your chest so your heart rises. Place your feet parallel. Hold your breath steady.

Enjoy holding the pose for one or two minutes as you embody your mantra with breath and body, and in the mental space that you're holding as you repeat the written mantra that's before you.

When the one to two minutes are over, place your hands together in front of your heart and aloud say, "Shanti. Namaste. Svaha." To me, these Sanskrit words mirror the sentiment, "Live the light within and see it within everyone. Peace is in reach. Peace can be now. And so it is. So be it."

CHAPTER 33

How to Use Language
as Your Liberator

⚶

ONLY BY GRAPPLING FOR WORDS in my writing career and learning how to select each one as carefully as humanly possible have I gotten a glimpse into why and how our language either defines or denies us. We either limit or liberate ourselves through the words that we use and oftentimes without even meaning to! It is only when we first explore the role of being conscious decision makers that we can gracefully transition from being mindless communicators to mindful co-creators of our lives and circumstances.

We cannot cast a magic spell that dictates how people are going to act towards us, but we can liberate ourselves from cycles of reaction that numb us from the inside out. These are the habitual cycles that we have for some reason leaned towards even though they are cycles that do not yield a great enough reward for us or provide us with the lives that we deserve. Whatever kind of car we drive, whatever size house we live in, whatever carat diamond ring we wear, we universally deserve to experience peace *within ourselves* and to have the skills we need to be proactive co-creators of our individual lives.

Despite any traumatic event that has happened to us that was beyond our control, we must desire to see ourselves beyond the pain in order to initiate recovery. Beneath the challenging feelings that the traumatic event has conjured up, within each of us, lives the survivor *we are meant to be.* And eventually, the thriver. The same person who is capable of moving *through* the storm is, in fact, *within* the storm.

My question is this: How can language assist us in weathering our storms in such a way that there are joyful tears on our cheeks and smiles on our lips?

LANGUAGE THAT CAUSES DRAMA

Here are five examples of phrases that often instigate drama.

* Right/wrong
* Better/worse
* But
* Should
* I have to
* You know?

Unless you're saying that you are wrong or incorrect, then avoid saying that other people are. Going to great lengths to let someone else know that he or she is wrong or incorrect isn't going to do anyone justice or get you the results that you want. *It will only create drama.* Trying to persuade others to change their thoughts and actions (especially those who have not asked for your advice or opinion) is a waste of your valuable energy. It's a loss *for you.*

In 2003, when I first attended Esalen Institute in Big Sur, California, everyone was talking about the word *should*. It was the consensus that the projecting of the word *should* onto someone else is offensive to the soulful operation of that person's free will. The word *should* was also found to be offensive in relation to what is possible in the realm of our personal imaginations and the fulfillment of our individual human potential.

"You should go to do _____! It's the best option *for you!"* When unsolicited this kind of phrase is an offense to other people when you say

it. Everyone has her or his own experience. The bottom line is that there are ways to dialogue with someone that get more favorable responses to cultivate bonding than to tell them *or insinuate* what they should or *shouldn't* be doing. For instance, if you were to instead say: "When I saw you do _____, *I wondered if* _____ was perhaps the best idea yet."

Alternatively, you might say: *"I want_____."* The blank space is where you insert the word that best expresses your desire for a particular type of experience. Not for what you want or think other people *should* do.

You might also try the old gem: *"May I suggest that _____?"* Suggesting something without expecting another person to do as you say promotes a drama-free environment.

This approach introduces a new way of doing something while not being domineering by saying what someone *should* do, or comparing your idea to the other's and saying that *yours* is a *better* idea.

The words *better* and *worse* are instigators. For example: "I thought that you could do *better*" or "I don't think that this can get any worse." *Better* and *worse* are ideas constructed from judgments, and the problem with yesterday's judgments carrying over to today, of course, is that neither you nor the world are as you once were.

The reason why we can walk the same path or drive the same road each day *and* have a different experience is that every moment we are in a new space-time continuum. It's impossible to experience something twice exactly the same way. No matter how similar outward conditions are, we are different the second time around. Often we're looking for new and different things, too.

The word *different* is actually the solution to constantly getting sucked into the thought that someone or something is *better* or *worse* than you and the work or experiences that you produce. Endless comparison goes on between past self and present self, as well as between self and others. The term we want to explore is *different than,* without any condescension in our tone. Ultimately, we want pure acceptance of different.

Is something *better* than something else or is someone more than someone else? It depends on who is doing the judging and what that individual's life experiences are. Whatever it is (or whomever we are thinking about), we can be sure that it is definitely *different than* something (or someone) else. You can always create more agreement and diminish judgment by using this term.

Let's move on to the word *but,* which is often used as a substitute for: *"Everything I just said is relevant and true, but . . . now I'll just tell you what I really think or want."*

"I really like you, *but* _____." (It's probably a negative.)

"I want to go, *but* _____." (It's probably an excuse to say no.)

The word *but* cancels out all the words placed before it all too often. It also contradicts everything that we've just said. For these reasons, it confuses the listener and works against securing what we really mean as speakers and co-creators of both our individual and shared universes.

The truth is that we are multifaceted people and one sentence is never going to articulate all that it is that we are trying to say. This is the reason why misunderstandings are a catalyst for drama.

Using the word <u>*and*</u> to replace <u>*but*</u> not only has the potential of clearing up many of our communication problems, it also allows us to stand taller and stronger. It takes courage to say what you really mean *and* it can shave away years of heartache, indecision, and misunderstanding when you begin to do so.

Let's imagine a romantic relationship where the commitment levels are uncertain. One partner says to the other, "I really like you, *but* . . . I don't know what to do." That does absolutely nothing to create intimacy. It doesn't remove the speaker from the relationship *or* keep the speaker in it. It's noncommittal. Most people listening to this would not feel motivated to remain in the relationship, and the word *but* is the main culprit.

Rather, what if this person said, "I really like you *and* I just don't know what to do." This is far more vulnerable and a supportive way of continuing the conversation. People who hear this are more likely to respond constructively because the person taking the time to communicate at least sounds "all in." In response, they may ask, "What's going on?" "What are you feeling?" or "What are you confused about?"

Let's move on to the phrase *have to* versus *want to*. *Have to* is the problem in the face of living a genuine, truly intentional, grateful and meaningful, life . . . or not. *Want to,* on the other hand, is the solution.

Imagine an elderly woman, for a moment, who is stomping around the house as if she's carrying bricks on her back and reports to all, "Today I *have to* _____ and then I *have to* _____." The words are heavy with resentment. No one likely knows what or who she is resenting. They only know that they feel like they're contributing to her burden when they're around. When people offer to help she rejects the offer. She is not fun to be around and she senses it, but doesn't know why.

Do you want to know how she evolved to perceive life as a resentment versus a celebration more days than not? The truth is that this woman was a rock for her family and had too much responsibility for too many years piled atop her shoulders. Her husband was ailing for most of their children's upbringing and she worked while he collected unemployment insurance. To top it off, she had two boys and always wanted a girl. There were things in her life that she had not yet come to peace with or forgiven.

Although the woman has been widowed for many years and is no longer the caretaker for her adult children, and although she doesn't work anymore, within herself she believes life to be all punishing. To her, life has always been a sort of punishment where things *have to* be done versus quietly appreciating the tasks for what they are and happily taking responsibility for the ones that are left.

One day, I said to this woman, "Really, do you *have to?*" after she had rattled off her self-created list of daily chores. "Is there anything you *like* about doing them?" I asked.

"Well, they're what make my world go around. My day is not all that exciting, but at least my to-do list gives me something to do."

This was an opportunity for the woman, who still had plenty of years to live, to exchange *have to* for *want to.* Before she knew it, she was more aware of her active choices while deciding to integrate more enjoyment into her life, too. Did she *want* to save for classes at the local dance studio? Did she *want* to take an afternoon stroll in the sunlight?

Changing her vocabulary helped her admit that she had been unaware of how much her laboured past had shaped her openness (or lack thereof) to having fun doing things she hadn't been able to do for two decades because of her unusual family caretaking obligations. In essence, she got her life back by making *one* conscious language shift.

To finish up, let's look at the expression *you know*. I'd been certain until recently that this phrase had dropped off of the face of the planet. But just because one person has stopped saying it doesn't mean that it's not still out there. As I sat on the patio of my local Whole Foods Market earlier this summer, a lady sitting behind me, who was speaking on her cell phone, ended every single sentence with, *"You know?"* More often than not, she didn't pause more than a fraction of a second to listen for the response from the person on the other end of the phone line.

Following every sentence with *you know* feeds into the frame of mind that we require everyone to know exactly what we are talking about in order to be understood, or worse yet, *validated* by someone other than ourselves. The worst part was that this woman talked on and on for five minutes without stopping which signaled to me that she was also afraid of truly being witnessed because she never gave the person on the other end the opportunity to connect to what she was saying.

Is it possible that *"You know?"* is also a cover for when we are afraid of being rejected and therefore do not create the space for other people to respond?

The next time you hear yourself asking, "You know?" stop yourself and request that the person you are speaking with say the following sentence to you: "No, I don't know *and I still love you*" or "No, I don't know *and I still like you*" depending on the depth and involvement of the friendship or relationship. When you do this you will feel most comfortable with either *like* or *love*. It's your choice. The focus here is to permit yourself both *not to know* if everyone understands *every inner working of your mind* AND to allow yourself enough space to step into your own power. Remember to thank your acquaintance for humoring you.

After doing the preceding exercise, notice that there is now a space of quiet in your speech patterns where those two words once were. *Allow* yourself to step into that space *and own* your positive personal power. If you're living the truly unique life that you deserve then not *everyone* will understand *everything* that you are saying *as your experience will be slightly different from theirs.*

That's okay.

When we speak like victims, we create trauma drama, whereas when we shift our language, we open new doors of satisfyingly enlightened possibility.

CHAPTER 34

How to Integrate Trauma-based Experiences

෯

FOR YOUR OPTIMAL HEALING AND growth, you must discover ways to integrate each of the experiences you've had that is trauma based. Use this exercise to investigate how you can grow as a result of your trauma.

STEP 1: BECOME STILL AND ROOTED

Tune in to the following mantra as you focus on your breath moving in and out of your body from the origin of your navel point. As you reach the end of the mantra, begin it again, from the top. Repeat the mantra two to six times. You may either silently think each of the focuses in the mantra or speak it aloud.

Inhale and think or say: "I am here."
Exhale and think or say: "Now."
Inhale: "I am safe."
Exhale: "Now."
Inhale: "I am in the present."
Exhale: "Now."

STEP 2: GO DEEPER

Write the following headings on a piece of paper, leaving blank space between them to capture your thoughts.

* Pre-Trauma Mental Climate:
* Pre-Trauma Emotional Climate:
* Pre-Trauma Physical Climate:
* Pre-Trauma Spirit Climate:

Then, contemplate and jot down *how you felt, what you thought* and perceived *before* the trauma. Choose one traumatic experience to focus on and reflect on at a time. Think about how you were *overall* before the event, mentally, emotionally, physically and spiritually.

For this exercise, consider the spirit part of you as the part of you that *perceives and is capable of understanding the big picture.* The spirit component of yourself is the eagle of the whole self. It is watchful and intuitive for the big picture and your purpose in this world. It senses the world around you.

STEP 3: BEGIN TO INTEGRATE

Now, write the following headings on a piece of paper, leaving blank space between them to capture your thoughts.

* Today's Mental Climate:
* Today's Emotional Climate:
* Today's Physical Climate:
* Today's Spirit Climate

Then, jot down your thoughts and feelings, and describe how you feel (emotional); see (spiritual); think (mental); and be and move (physical) within the world today. Do not think to focus only on how you have been affected by the trauma. Rather, without focusing on the effects of the trauma, explain the climate you live in today. Do not overthink your responses on how you've been affected. Instead, simply listen for the answers as they come and detail how you are existing in your today.

STEP 4: COMPARE YOUR LISTS

Now, take as long as you require to write in your journal about the differences that you notice between your two lists.

Ask yourself this question.

How does my pre-trauma self differ from my post-trauma self?

STEP 5: ACCEPT AND LET GO

Finally, take a piece of paper, either ripped from your notebook or a loose leaf, and fold it so that there is a dividing line down the center of the page. Write *"Accept"* on the left side and *"Let Go"* on the right side.

It's time to answer the next question. Which answers will you *accept*? And, which changes will you *let go* in relation to the answers that you have discovered connected to the Step 4 question: How does my pre-trauma self differ from my post-trauma self?

You may read the note below, "Expanding on Spirit," either before or after you complete this step. If you are overflowing with ideas, then please begin writing first. Otherwise, pause and take a moment to gain more wisdom and insight by reading the note.

EXPANDING ON SPIRIT. . .

Spirit is what you think is possible in the world in general. It is beyond the ego's limited focus on particular people and places as being the only reality, only solution, or only problem. Spirit is the part of us that is capable of viewing the world in its entirety. It is the part of us that is willing to look at life in its wholeness in order to feel and create possibilities. It is, therefore, a very powerful source of healing after trauma.

I hope this explanation helps you in completing the final step of your exploration and discovery exercise.

What does living with a healthy spirit mean to you?

What is its potential?

STEP 6: EMBODY THE GREATEST OUTCOME

Within the self, as we are now more aware of than ever, are many aspects and elements that are in some ways beyond comprehension. I have heard that some first-responders and emergency medical technicians are trained to use a technique of so-called emotional first-aid to assist trauma victims on scene when they arrive. In order to soothe the patient's nervous system, they whisper into the left ear, which activates the right hemisphere of the brain, saying phrases such as, "Everything is going to be OK." This approach initiates healing.

There are many ways to address the unspoken, feeling parts of us that can accelerate healing and remedy past unhealthy misperceptions about whom we are, why we are here on this planet, and what we want to do about it. The next step is one of these ways.

For this step, I invite you to keep an open mind.

You will now take the options from the column marked "Accept" on the list you made in Step 5 and turn them into fully written out affirmative phrases. For instance, if one of the points in your accept column, was *"I now know how to say 'No' more than I did before."* Then, growing that into a full-fledged sentence that serves as an affirmative phrase is your objective.

In this case, the affirmative phrase will be something to the effect of: *"Saying NO when it is necessary in my life gives me great strength"* or *"My ability to say NO helps me clarify what I am saying YES to."*

Once you have turned each point in your "Accept" column into an affirmative phrase, turn on a recording device.

Once you've recorded your affirmative phrases, place the recording device next to your left ear. Play back your recording so that the right hemisphere of your brain can be stimulated and included in this whole-being exercise. The right brain is the doorway to the empathic, highly-intelligent *feeling*-self. This feeling-self must be involved in all mental shifts or else the mental shift alone won't be enough to create the profound shifts that you are after.

Listen to the recording of your affirmations as often as you like.

I hope that you enjoy integrating the new thoughts and ideas that you have taken the time to write down into your journey of recovery.

BONUS STEP: PUT YOUR VISION IN ACTION

As a bonus step in this process, think of something you can do within the next twenty-four hours to enact your vision of high spirit and purpose, and then do it! A symbolic gesture is needed to anchor the vision in your reality.

If it doesn't feel too personal and private, you may ask a friend to take a photo of you enacting the feeling of what living with high purpose and spirit means to you. Please make sure to post this picture on the wall or refrigerator door, or somewhere else that you can see it on a daily basis, during your period of great transformation as you set your sails to conquer your one-of-a-kind trauma drama!

Whatever you discovered were the realities of your trauma *are yours* and no one else's. Yours to heal. Yours to love. Yours to ultimately transcend.

Whenever the past begins to feel bigger than your present goals and dreams and preferred reality, use your affirmations as an anchor. If and when the past is sneaking up and you feel like you're not sure how you can let go of intruding unpleasant feelings and/or thoughts, replay the recording next to your left ear.

Here is an affirmation that came to me during a particularly rough patch in my life. I still like to use it today:

"This is but a small deal in the face of where I am going."

Repeating an affirmative phrase, such as this one, can help to ground you in your strength, accept the difficulties you face today, and put your focus on the present.

CHAPTER 35

How to Get the Universe to Yield to You

❦

How valuable to you is it to know how to summon *your* inner strength? Just as importantly, if you knew that looking for the hidden gifts in life's grueling challenges is the best way to do this, might you begin your search right now? I sure hope so.

When I was going through a particularly challenging time, I can recall how I sat down quietly and allowed myself to feel the gravity of the situation. I also allowed myself to feel what *might shift* or *needed to shift* within me in order to know that the situation was over. I made this discovery by asking, "What needs to happen *inside me* for *me* to know that all is well, again?"

Before that day, I had generally looked at situations through the lens of what needed to happen outside of me in order for me to feel okay. This time I was looking within for my answers, during an imposed quiet moment of my day, with my eyes gently closed.

I began to focus on the physical sensations below skin level, and then on the sensations in the space around me that lay just off of my skin. My mind observed my body's state of being without desiring or attempting to change anything. Even more rewarding was that I chose not to give names to anything my body and mind were feeling. It was a real blessing to allow the experience without needing or even wanting to assess what it was in words *or* in previously discerned perceptions of what the elements comprising my experience in that moment meant.

Then I began to imagine all the people who were involved in the situation that was troubling me. I imagined them outside of the behaviors that were challenging me in that present moment. To do so brought incredible peace and a compassionate mind. I felt more resilient and empowered to act on my own behalf after acknowledging the existence of these people outside of how I knew them and instead I visualised them sitting around the coffee table with their families, cooking, hiking, or in short, *being* outside of how I knew them—and being *with joy and love.*

ENTER COMPASSION'S IMAGINATION

For a moment, imagine someone who you may not have an open line of communication with and who may have perceptions of you that are not in alignment with the truth and love that you live and know to be your life. This may be easy to do, as people are constantly projecting on one another and often come into relationship from a place of fear that facilitates disruption. Many people block the possibility of having a healthy camaraderie between the self and others with their self-imposed drama without even knowing it.

Now, please try the following: Close your eyes and then imagine seeing the individual you that have chosen to focus on outside of the context that you are familiar with today. If it is your colleague, imagine the person at a community ice skating rink with family. The person who is your challenge is also a mother and/or a sister, or a brother in need of more love, understanding or general compassion in life.

If it is difficult to imagine someone as having a positive role in a family or in the lives of the people she knows today, then imagine the person as a miniature version of herself, as a preschooler, thirty years ago, meeting school peers for the very first time. Might you imagine the desire of this individual to be loved and/or have companionship? It might be attainable to imagine the person as a four-year-old or a five-year-old in this scenario.

Take a mental snapshot of the person as you see her being a small child self.

Pause then, and with your eyes mostly or all the way closed, repeat this compassion mantra: *Om Tare Tuttare Tureh Svaha.*

In some cultures, Tara is known as a goddess of compassion. I personally think of the words as I say the mantra as being the starting point of the creation of powerful energy that helps bring the internal sense of compassion into my day. I said this mantra every day for four years, along with other mantras spoken in a foreign tongue, in order to move beyond my mental prisons of *good* and *bad, forgivable* and *unforgivable.* This trained me to bring freedom from *and forgiveness for* moments and people I didn't understand to the reality of my everyday.

To participate in the creation of our reality is crucial for our well-being. Just because someone is angry with you because of ideas they have constructed in their own mind does not mean that your reality has to be anger, too. This mantra helps return you to the quiet and all-fulfilling wisdom of compassion that has existed long before we were born.

The practice of saying the mantra 108 times, as yoga practitioners and meditators around the world do takes around ten minutes to complete. It is incredibly rejuvenating for body, mind, and spirit, and especially the mind as it gives the practitioner a break from experiencing the overly logical, often repetitive, and cyclical nature of the mind.

If the words of the mantra I'm suggesting are too foreign for you to remember, or appreciate, then go to YouTube and search for a sung version of the *Om Tare Tuttare Tureh Svaha* mantra that you like most and follow along with a video of someone repeating it as you listen. When you feel able, repeat the sung mantra along with them. (If you join my seven-week course on resilience ask me to tell you my favourite one!)

Once you have completed the mantra, pull up the mental snapshot of the person you have chosen to focus on. Shift your awareness to the person, again, *outside of* how you know him or her.

Take ten full-body breaths while intending to focus on the vibrations in your body shifting and moving as result of saying the mantra 108 times and being consciously aware of this individual you have chosen to honor—even if you have not yet come close to understanding this person today.

Last step. Eyes closed, please. Inhale and draw in all the pain, sadness, frustration, and/or anger associated with the individual you are holding in mind, as you know him or her. Near the top of the inhalation, imagine also breathing in all the serenity and peace that exists as a counter experience to the aforementioned emotions. Allow this lightness to outshine the darkness of the heavier emotions, once you have acknowledged and not run from or pushed away those harder, darker emotions.

Pause before you exhale. Then, at the point of exhalation, allow the corners of your mouth to lift up. Take a moment to send waves of peace on the stream of your exhalation towards the compassionate mental image of the person you've chosen, which you are intentionally holding in mind for this practice. Focus on a feeling of peace both for you and that person.

MEANWHILE IN WASHINGTON. . .
Have you heard how practitioners of Transcendental Meditation in Washington, D.C., caused the crime rate to drop by 23 per cent when they were meditating as a group? Small groups of people expressing peaceful energy can produce waves of peace. *See the EndNotes at the back of this book for additional info on the subject.*

NEW CONSIDERATIONS. . .
Has anyone shared the Ho'oponopono Clearing Meditation from Hawaii with you, yet? This is another powerful technique to produce ripples of peace in your environment. See the EndNotes for where to learn more.

This is a powerful step on your journey to reclaiming your positive personal power to its fullest. *(Also, see EndNotes.)*

More on Mantras

When we practice this particular mantra technique, we can discover peace within our own minds *first*. Whether or not compassion comes through you for that particular person with ease afterwards, by discovering peace within yourself first you *will* increase the chances of drawing compassionate circumstances towards you moving forward in all of your interactions.

We cannot account for other people's behaviour. We do not need to focus on displeasing behaviour any more than we did in the moment of conflict or in the moment of actual trauma itself. In this practice, we surrender to whatever the universal tides bring next, and in doing so, deepen our trust in the present situation.

If trying the mantra is not for you, then reread this section before you go to sleep so that your subconscious mind can partake in one of the exercises as you rest overnight.

CHAPTER 36

How to Begin Shifting Your
Unconscious Mind Patterns Today

❧

FROM MY PERSONAL WORK OF recovery and self-mastery, as well as through my work of helping others to conquer trauma drama and thrive in their lives, I have become aware of the mind cycles we go through after trauma. The mind of the trauma survivor is prone to misinterpreting otherwise harmless feelings and mental states, and transforming the experience into something that seems life threatening. In studying my own personal reactions one day while I was out on a walk, I noticed that although I had been anticipating the next experience of the day I was on the brink of the body-feeling experience of deeply rooted and irrational fear. Moments later, my mood shifted and I noticed myself thinking about how excited I was about the day ahead—and yet, within that excitement was a great deal of anxiety, too. There was nothing real to fear in that moment of walking down a quiet and peaceful neighborhood lane. Nonetheless, I felt afraid.

As I continued to walk along, I realized that I'd had few experiences over the years when my body-feeling self hadn't automatically translated otherwise healthy anticipation *into fear,* or muddled excitement *into anxiety.* For approximately twenty-four months after my experience in New York City, my mind had been responding to physical signals of anticipation *and* excitement as if they were threats. Excitement became its naughty sister aka anxiety and healthy anticipation became dread and fear. It took me quite a while to recognize that this was happening outside of my conscious awareness. In fact, the realization I made on that day as I strolled in the pristine British Columbia neighborhood would become quite the eye opener.

I had literally been tripping out without warrant!

Whereas the body is a loyal friend that communicates to us when there is danger in the immediate area that we need to attend to, if the physical body has not healed from the experience of trauma it can and will send incorrect messages to the subconscious mind, informing it of nonexistent dangers. Thus, we react when we don't have to. This kind of triggering is the fundamental damage to our mental "circuitry" that causes trauma drama.

Did you know that although the subconscious mind heavily influences the conscious mind, the conscious mind can similarly influence and eventually change the "programming" of the otherwise dominating subconscious mind with the right amount of continued effort and intention?

It can!

By focusing on how you want to retrain your brain, and with repetition, you can teach it to react differently to stimuli in the environment. That's also how you can begin to master your emotions. Waking up early and also as the last activity before sleeping, you can speak your desired suggestions and the subconscious mind will heed the call. When brainwaves are in alpha, the state of relaxation accessible through meditation, the dominating beliefs and patterns implanted in our minds at impressionable times of our lives (including when we were kids, as well as times when we were highly vulnerable) are more easily shifted (and eventually changed) by this practice of repetition.

You might already know all of the above or this may be new to you. In either case, I encourage you to take this information and run with it tonight before bed. The sooner you begin supporting your healing with positive thoughts that eventually lead to beliefs, the sooner you'll get relief from your triggers.

What can be done when we're in an innocuous moment and suddenly experience irrational fear or anxiety? Well, that answer cannot be given in one quick, tidy sentence. For certain we want to breathe and ground ourselves as much as possible. We also need to create as much safety in the conditions around us as we can.

Those are both effective short-term solutions.

In addition, we need to take a long-term approach. The brain needs to reprogram itself so that it can experience anticipation as *anticipation* again and excitement as *excitement!* To support the running of new programs in the mind, we must learn to use the power of the brain to focus *and create* new thoughts that are unique to our lives and essentially learn to trust life, again. Trust life's flow. Its ups and downs. Its ease . . . its hardships . . . its challenges.

Embrace the Challenge. . .

It's important to remember that the brain and the mind are two different things. By using the brain to create anew we give the mind that follows the brain's suggestions new tracks around which to run, play and explore!

What else can we do to dissipate states of anxiety and fear?

Simply put: We need to stare them in the face. We cannot run from the thoughts or feelings that arise as they do so. If we do, they will rule us.

What do I mean by *run from thoughts and feelings?* I mean avoid them. I mean try to block them. I also mean deny that they're happening. If we allow ourselves to follow the path of resisting our fears and anxieties they will build in strength and challenge our ability to exist in a healthy, rewarding life.

By *not running* I am not advising that you make up some elaborate story about your fear and anxiety or tell everyone you know how triggered you feel, as if these are the most profound experiences that you've had all day. I mean to *experience* them in that moment, for what they are . . . *and then move on!*

Patience is a virtue. Especially when pertaining to ourselves.

What we look in the eyes loses its power and its hold on us.

The secret in this lesson is in *feeling*.

What is being described here is a 100 per cent feeling-based technique.

To allow yourself openness with your deep-seated *body-based* feelings is to dissipate them with something akin to the power of the sun.

CONSIDER TAKING ACTION TODAY

Take a moment and write down on a blank piece of paper, *"I am safe."* Place the paper with this message in front of you on a table, or if you are sitting on the floor, on the floor before you.

Now close your eyes. Think of something that scares you. Something **not** associated with your trauma, yet one of your core fears—rational or irrational, "silly" or intense.

Shine the light of your awareness on the body-feeling that you notice when thinking of this fear. Remember that you are safe in this moment. Make a note of where you feel the fear in your body. Have the intention to be non-reactive: *You do not need to do anything about this fear.* Watch the feeling as if you are energetically staring it in its face for seven slow inhalations and seven slow exhalations. If you have difficulty breathing slowly, ask someone to remind you to breathe slowly or record your voice for playback saying, "Now breathe in slowly once . . . Breathe out slowly once . . . Now, breathe in slowly twice . . . Breathe out slowly twice . . . ," and so on. Any recorder or smartphone (or possibly a free downloadable app) can record your voice as a reminder so you can do this exercise whenever you want. Make sure to honor that you must feel *100 percent* safe in your surroundings so that your belief factor *and knowing* that you are safe runs high.

Once you have done the above, pick up this book again and continue to the next step.

As you watched the body-feeling, neither denying it nor reacting to it, did you notice that within a matter of seconds it was no longer in existence? Was your mind as clear as it was before you first conjured up the thought and image of your chosen fear?

Begin to focus on your body again with a neutral awareness, experiencing it for this moment without aiming to change any part of the experience. It is likely that thinking about the fear that you chose to introduce caused some tension or discomfort in your body. So begin to invite the body to let go of the tensions. Feel the muscles softening around the largest bones in your legs. Feel your shoulders drop again. Invite your throat muscles and tongue to soften. Feel your breath move in your low belly.

This practice of intentionally *inviting* fear into your moment's experience and then intentionally *returning* the body to a place of well-being will decrease the length of time that you feel stuck when experiencing hardship.

After all, being a victim is the experience of being stuck within a situation. In the here and now, when you're safe, you do not have to be a victim, anymore. It is possible, that feeling stuck *can be a signal* that it's a great time to take action and move forward.

CHAPTER 37

How to Shift from Chronic Over-Explainer Mode

༉

WE DO NOT ALWAYS NEED to name things. In fact, practice not-naming. The next time something is bothering you, have awareness of what it is—yes—but say no to naming it, because naming things ignites a story. Naming promotes more focus and awareness *on what's disagreeable to you.* That's the last thing you need as what we focus on and are most aware of quickly becomes our reality.

Refusing to name something does not show ignorance, insensitivity or laziness. In fact, it is *wise* to refrain from announcing every detail of what you are experiencing day in and day out. If someone you spend time with has to know *why* regarding every action or word you choose then it is more than likely their problem of control.

There are ways to work around wanting to make changes without going into too much detail about why. For instance, if you come across someone who does not rub you the right way, rather than spending hours figuring out what it is that you do not like or how your perspective of them or of a disagreeable situation must be correct, say, "There's something about this individual that does not agree with me." The simplification is true, yet you're *not* overfeeding whatever the problem is.

Over-explaining reinforces the problem.

In the event that something in your immediate environment is compromising one of your core values and you decide that you need to honor the awareness of this by temporarily leaving the environment altogether, instead of reciting a long list of what it is you do not like say, "I'm ready to change environments as soon as possible." Or, "I'm ready to shift from this part of our day together if that's okay."

Or, "Let's move on to something else."

Do you see how you can be authentic by speaking about your experience *versus speaking poorly about yourself or other people* while maintaining your commitment to *reduce* drama and maintain a happy state of mind and an environment filled with people and things that are nourishing for you?

Reduce drama. *Be a mystery.*

CHAPTER 38

How to Do The Vision Feel Technique

✵

THE VISION FEEL TECHNIQUE IS a practice in which we use visual props to remind us of our intentions. We also practice speaking our deepest, innermost truths aloud so that we may increase the likelihood of stepping into those realities on a daily basis. And, soon! There are two reasons this exercise is great. First, it enables us to embody and project the power of our intentions all on our own. Second, this exercise helps us become content *now* while also helping us build towards the ultimate life of our dreams.

You'll want to give yourself a fair amount of time to implement this technique because it has several phases.

To begin this exercise, you need to record some of your affirmations that you've written based upon your reading in earlier chapters. You can record them on a cellular phone or through any online service that gives you the capacity to create MP3s for free. (See EndNotes at the back of this book.)

You will likely want to have notepaper and a pen at hand in case you want to make notes. You'll also need some art supplies for Step 3, in which you'll be invited to make a vision board. Those might include already read magazines that can be torn and cut up, scissors, crayons, colored markers or pencils, and computer paper.

Once you have your recorded affirmations ready assume a comfortable seated or supine position. *Feel free to use affirmations that may have resonated with you from the BONUS MATERIAL following Chapter 21 of this book.* Now, gently close your eyes halfway and invite your eye muscles to soften so the room and the objects in it become a blur. You may also choose to close your eyes entirely. Push the PLAY button on your recording device and begin to listen to the affirmations that you have chosen to speak and prerecord.

Step 1: Listen to the sound of the affirmations and as you listen notice what encouraging and happy visions or images come to you. Focus on the enjoyable feelings that are being produced because of the affirmations playing as well as on expanding the positive feeling rather than simply repeating the affirmations you hear. *Cultivating the feeling is what makes the Vision Feel Technique effective.*

Step 2: When you're finished listening to the recording, stop for anywhere between thirty seconds to an entire five minutes to make a few quick notes of the visions/images that arose alongside their related appropriate feelings that you were either conjuring up as you listened or that naturally existed as a byproduct of allowing light, buoyant and expansive feelings to enter into this contemplative moment.

Step 3: As you continue to increase the life-giving feelings you've just created by closely focusing on the words of the affirmations, create a vision board that brings your vision *to life!* Find images in magazines that represent the visions you've just had. Then, cut them out and tape them to construction paper, or paint or draw images that most represent the vision you have for *your* life.

Step 4: Return to your comfortable seated or supine position and turn on the recorded affirmations and listen to them from the beginning again. Post or prop up the vision board you made where you can see it. If you're lying down, turn on your side so that you can see it propped up against the wall, dresser, table, or bed. Keep your gaze relaxed. Have your eyes closed or halfway closed so that the primary sense of your eyesight does not dominate the moment by making you overly attached to your current circumstances. You want to be able to remain in your self-created, safe, imagined world without becoming distracted by details in the room outside of the vision board you have made.

Remember, dreams DO come true!

As you conjure up life-giving and life-supportive feelings, begin looking at the visual replicas of what your inner eye has shown it wants most for you.

In our daily lives, between billboards, magazines, and newspapers, we are regularly inundated with images—not to mention the memories of our past—so it is a **must** to stay connected to the images that most support your *inner* vision (not the ones being fed to you by others) and build you up *right now!*

If the idea of getting what you want in the blink of an eye scares you, be patient with yourself. Even though you know what fear is and are familiar with fear, you are also aware of what it is like to overcome obstacles, beat the odds, and set your mind to accomplishing something that perhaps no one else believes you can. *Stay with it.* The rewards are worth it.

Are you ready to clearly affirm what you want?

Well . . . ? *What is it?*

Only you know best.

Today is *your* day to shift from victim to victor in yet another way!

p.s. Make sure to view your vision board before closing your eyes to rest at night and first thing in the morning when you're reciting your affirmations *either silently or aloud!*

CHAPTER 39

How to Benefit From Self-Dialogue

༄

HOW OFTEN DO WE HEAR doomsday questions, such as, *"I can't imagine anything good coming of this—can you?"*

Granted, weighing of pros and cons for all kinds of future actions is essential, yet the types of questions we ask either positively assume or negate our ability to create valuable experiences in life. There was a time in my own life when I thought the root of all suffering began with the phrase, *"I want ____."* You can fill in the blank with one of your own desires. I had thought that wanting *so much, and so often* would threaten my embodiment of spirit and prevent me from enjoying the simple, soulful, things in life that were before me. Then I woke up to the fact that we are not meant to suffer and that happiness is a byproduct of being in alignment with our values and asking for what it is we want *even if we do not get it.* Happiness is the *anticipation* of what we want. Frustrated, disappointed, sadness is the outcome of *expecting* what we want.

As you continue reading this chapter and the rest of the book, rely on your desire to want *what you want* and to believe that your happiness and your growth to new levels is a byproduct of allowing yourself to plan, dream, and revise the habitual way you speak, feel, think and act on a daily basis.

The next time you realize that the phrasing of a question, or questions, is setting you up to assume defeat, pause for a moment to ask: *"Is this question geared for my highest well-being?"*

Ask: "Is the commentary running through my head right now for my highest well-being?"

Ask: "If I shift my angle that I am looking at this from, what will, without a doubt, happen?"

In the event that you're not comfortable with your emotional experience in the moment, ask: "If I could pick any emotion right now, what would I pick *and why?*"

In any situation where your trust in the world, in the universe, in God is being challenged and you find that you are at the bottom of the emotional barrel, ask, "Is this feeling or emotion that I've either consciously or unconsciously chosen for my highest well-being?"

If the answer is yes, that's great. Follow up by asking, "What can I do to reinforce this emotion, *right now?*"

If the answer is no, that's all right. Just ask: **"What will it take for me to want to evolve into a more nourishing state, feeling, or emotion on this new day?"**

CHAPTER 40

How to Shift from Victim to Victor

༆

Is *VICTIM* A BAD WORD? No, it's not. It's simply a description of one of the realities that we possess within ourselves. Part of my truth is that I will always be a victim of rape, a survivor of rape, and a thriver after rape.

A thriver is a victor. The state between victim and victor is the state of being a *survivor*. When something horrible happens, like the earthquakes that leveled Nepal to rubble not once, but twice, in 2015, or the tsunami that hit Thailand in 2004, and we get through it, we may scream, "Yay! I survived!" We feel relief and we may also feel some guilt if others have been harmed instead of us. Think about people who survived the sinking of *The Titanic*, a supposedly unsinkable boat that famously struck an iceberg on its maiden voyage in 1912. Many survived being victims of the crew ship's negligence as they found their way to lifeboats. Roughly 1,500 people perished. Do you think that they may have felt both relief and guilt when the chaos was over?

As we start to move forward to have realizations about the *life-giving* part of our trauma, we are on the path to thriving. What is meant by *life-giving*? There are certain ways that we may begin to look at traumatic events that give us enough perspective on them that our ability to co-create our next, deeply rewarding experience in life is within reach and knowingly possible, again. We are suddenly able to see that even a horrible event was only what it was . . . an experience in our lives.

Even our initial response to trauma, on some level, was meant to be. Our darkest experiences are capable of pulling something beautiful and courageous out of us that restores our sense of wholeness. Latent strengths and talents emerge that eventually make us more resilient as our recovery progresses and we create newfound purpose and meaning in our lives.

In my own life, I have had the realization that it was because of my kidnapping and rape that I was able to bravely leave behind all I had known in order to move to a new country and pursue the path of the healing arts on newer and richer levels. Putting a safe distance between the crime scene and my new place of study was what I wanted and needed in order to feel safe and nurtured by my environment. I still visited the United States on a biyearly basis, yet knowing that there was new soil on which to grow and learn felt right for me. Furthermore, I wouldn't have taken off across the continent to devote so much time to deepening my healing practice if it weren't for the events I experienced as a teenager.

The bottom line that I want you to understand is this: The moment we can see the good that has come about because we survived, we are, in fact, on the road to thriving in our lives once again and becoming a victor.

Being a victim, a survivor, or a victor is a matter of subjective experience.

Each of us has all three of these characters and perspectives inside of us. We are never one of the three permanently, no matter what family we come from, who we know, or how much money we have. Each of us constantly shifts between these three states of being and self-images throughout different stages of our lives. For instance, an intrinsic component of being a victim is having something unexpected happen. We are not ready for whatever the circumstance may be. With the element of surprise comes utter shock. In that moment, we are victims. Therefore, each one of us who shares the common thread of vulnerability in their human nature cannot and will not escape being victimized at one point or another. It is human, after all.

Now, do we walk around screaming at the top of our lungs that we're victims or vulnerable? Probably not. In fact, in thirty-two years I have never seen anyone do so in public. However, even the most thick-skinned individual has been and likely will be a victim again in his life. Let's hope this is the case, as if we are not susceptible to being victims, we are not putting our feet out the door in the morning and living.

The point is not to judge when you are a victim: Judging ourselves takes a whole lot of energy and a whole lot of time! It delays the healing process and thus slows the transition to the newly realized place of survivor, and eventual victor.

The essential part of shifting from victim to victor is recognizing the symptoms of trauma and knowing how to treat them with greater command and diligence each and every time. Let's say that a man wants to go to die and go to heaven because he's heard so much about it, but he doesn't believe in suicide. Let's say that this guy also does not believe that he was chosen to be born, but that it was disastrous "mistake." This means he wakes up every day wishing he hadn't been born and feeling victimized by being alive. *If only it weren't for my parents,* he thinks.

Let's say that this man came to me and in earnest told me he wanted to do his best to overcome the resentment he felt every morning as he awoke. He wanted to learn how to shift from victim to survivor to thriver because he'd become so miserable that he was considering the unforgivable act of taking his own life. What do you think could be done to help this man shift from being a helpless victimized human to a victorious survivor of ill-thoughts and beliefs, and begin to tackle life?

One of the best actions I could take with such a man would be to ask him what he thought he would like most about this place called *heaven.* Why? Well, a significant portion of crafting our life stories comes from observing where we choose to live within our thoughts. Of course, if we do not evaluate what images we drift in and out of within our minds from day to day it is not a choice at all. We are simply living a model of what has been shown to us by the world without any questioning or curiosity. It is safe to say that if we aren't observing our thoughts, we are not partaking in the creation of them. For, if we aren't aware of what we are thinking then what is the motivation to change them at all?

If you, survivor, are observing your thoughts, you are the equivalent of a brave explorer who has set out on a sea of uncertainty. If you are unwilling to observe your thoughts, it is certain that nothing will change by your own will because your life will be running on autopilot. If you wish to have someone else create your life by her own suggestion and design your life's chances are you undoubtedly latching onto *her* thoughts as a way to see your life change? I can guarantee you that you will not be soulfully gratified by this approach as you might be *if* you start by ascertaining the direction of your own thoughts. By observing your mind you'll begin to see what you want to change. This indicates that you are a victor. And, it is only time before life yields your reward.

Survivors and victors do not fight where they are in their lives. They know the difference between states and stages. They know these moments to be stages of their lives and passing ones at that. They, therefore, stay focused on keeping their states of mind conducive to winning their inner battles with perseverance and with kindness to themselves.

Embrace your inner victim, survivor, and thriver and learn from them!

If you choose to live in victor mode, then focus on the people in society and among your family and/or friends whom you believe have learned to be victors themselves. If you are unaware of anyone in your life or environs who displays the qualities that *you* believe are victorious, then make a list of what qualities you think a victor would possess by looking farther afield, such as into movies or books—or just by using your imagination.

Whether you come up with a list of people or a list of direct qualities, focus on the list at least once a day for two minutes. You will ignite those qualities within yourself. This practice is best done first thing in the morning, because you are not yet caught up in events. You're most likely in action mode and not reaction mode as you are when you are replying to emails and phone calls. It's a great reminder of your intention to be victorious during the rest of the day.

There is a part of the brain that doesn't know the separation between you and others. This part of the brain sees joy in another and immediately causes you to feel it within yourself. This means that if we give to someone else, it is as good as giving to ourselves. That's why we feel great when we work for charity or support our friends and family--and even strangers! This part of our brains understands that we are as one. If you do not recognize this as being true it is only because somewhere along the line you have learned to see yourself as separate from the whole. Through conscious recognition of your connectedness with humanity this dated perception is capable of being changed, if you wish.

If you are uncertain of how to be brave or courageous or steadfast during a process of healing or empowerment, think of those who have displayed signs and traces of bravery before you. A large part of being at peace is feeling well. If these states of being are seemingly far off in the distance simply do your best to remain steadily aware of them rather than grasping for them. These ways of being are already a part of you if only for the simple fact that you have felt them within you as you recognized them in others. They have become part of your brain wiring and hold a potential for action.

The catch twenty-two is if you grasp for qualities you want to possess, like courage. In this case, you are likely to be blindsided by *what is actually happening* in the moment. Feeling sad or weak is ***not*** a negative. These emotions are teachers, and momentary stops on the journey. Their presence does not override the fact that all other emotions exist within you, too.

As we become *aware* of states of being versus *grasping* for them they can serve not only as tools for our personal growth, but springboard us into positive action. When we are attached to one state or another it becomes like baggage we carry around. No matter how good a state feels or appears to be, we must maintain neutrality. Observe your states of being without becoming attached to them so that you can be sure to remain connected to your *ever-changing* self as you naturally continue to shift and grow.

Being able to enjoy your life and proactively make changes is a victory, making you a *victor*.

THE GREATEST SURVIVOR'S MISTAKE

Trying to push the past away in order to be a victor is the greatest mistake a survivor can make. On the contrary if, we genuinely embrace the past it will wake up all the sleepy, neglectful, parts within us and cure the desire to run any longer. In total, we receive our whole selves back, victim and victor, and far exceed mere survival. When I was writing my first novel, I dated a man who introduced me to the perils of mental abuse. My mother and family friends thought he was the nicest. He was. To them. But when we were alone and no one was listening, to me he'd say things like, "I don't know who could be attracted to you." The strangest part was, in other moments he stood up *with me* against the mistreatment of women in the face of sexual abuse.

It wasn't until he exposed his own sexual abuse history, as a small boy at the hands of an hotelier who his mother had left him with as she went shopping for the day on their vacation in Europe that I realized he wasn't angry with me. He was scared of me and of being intimate with me because of the memories it conjured up for him. So his unnecessary self-defense was to bash me verbally in order to protect himself from having to be vulnerable in intimacy. He was not a bad person, yet his behavior and instant mood changes were not healthy for my personal growth and self-esteem.

My boyfriend ended up leaving his job after one of his bosses made physical advances towards me while he stood twenty-feet away. I continuously stepped in the opposite direction away from his employer as the man repeatedly stepped one step closer again and again. I chose to focus on the great courage it took for my boyfriend to reveal to his employer that the reason why I was not in attendance at the country club soiree the next week was because I didn't want to be around his boundary-crossing boss. A day later he quit because he didn't want to work for someone he couldn't respect.

Despite this noble move, this ex could not maintain his own personal integrity with his treatment of me with his words. I told him I had decided to leave and travel back to the city I was living in. I did not blame him and I did not try to change him beyond the changing of my relationship to him. Given all the contrasting experiences, some loving, some far from being so, I knew it would be a sad day to leave. Instead of pushing him away, or the experience, I literally and figuratively embraced him at the small airport where he dropped me off.

When it was time to go our separate ways, I pulled him near and kissed him harder and more passionately than I ever had before. It's not because things were always right between us, but because I knew in that moment that if I could embrace the moment with a physical action instead of pushing it away then it meant I could embrace the experience for what it was and therefore be free of it. I moved on, free of any victim mentality and immediately began enjoying the next phase of my life upon returning to my home town.

CHAPTER 41

How to Neutralize Your Thoughts

꙳

It is obvious that we have both toxic thoughts and positive, life-enhancing thoughts. But why do we so frequently jump from positive to negative? How is such a drastic shift in our mental mindset even possible? And is there anything we can do when we've suddenly flipped to the negative and want to get back to the positive?

Yes, in fact: we can learn how to embrace our *neutral* thoughts. We may know that it is mentally unhealthy *and unstable* to jump from, *"Life sucks!"* to *"Life is awesome!" A healthy brain needs a springboard upon which to shift. That springboard is your conscious use of the power of neutralizing thoughts.* As we create a bridge from negative to positive *we intentionally* participate in our personal individual shifts.

Let's say that you walk into your best friend's house and say, *"Life sucks!"* after you spent the whole day struggling with even the simplest tasks for whatever reason. You might be pretty upset if your friend looked at you and responded, *"Life is awesome!"* with a big smiling face and zero regard for where you are in that moment. You *might* perceive the friend as insensitive, uncaring about your current state, or even worse oblivious to what you're feeling in that moment. In this case, whether you're talking to your best friend or walking in your front door and you're the only one around, if you utter words that are akin to these then the first thing you want to do is identify *what* made it such a horrible day. Let's surmise that the day was horrible because you were triggered by one of your colleagues speaking poorly about another coworker.

When you think about why this is so upsetting to you, you will likely discover that it is because you do not have any control over the bad mouthing that is taking place. Not having *control* reminds you of a traumatic office experience where, in this instance, and for the sake of this fictitious story, you also did not have any control in.

Having uncovered the painful thought, you now realize that *you* can partake in a three-part affirmation-building process to let go of the trigger and reframe the experience so that there is a light at the end of the tunnel and you can see that you will move out and beyond this particularly triggering experience. This realization is necessary in order to come back to a place of equilibrium in situations where there are massive triggers in your day.

You may either write the following down or make a mental note of the following:

Step 1: Name the negative thought. In this example, "Life sucks!"

Step 2: Acknowledge the trigger. Whatever it was, acknowledge your trigger with this statement: "I am being triggered today." Notice we are *not* saying, It was "good" or "bad" that you had the experience of being triggered today. *We are being neutral here.* Simply, "I am being triggered today."

Step 3: Combine the two steps. "At times I think life sucks *and* I realize I am also being triggered right now."

We are acknowledging the negative thought pattern and the cause of it from neutral, *nonjudgmental* ground. Remember, we are not strictly our thoughts and behaviors *as with the spiritual path both of these change throughout our lives.* We are *vast* beings of potential who deserve to identify with our changeability versus past, outdated, thoughts and behaviors. In fact, the more we also see other people's thoughts and behaviors as *part* of them while at the same time not being *who they are* we widen the path as that many more people can walk beside us on our spiritual journeys.

Are we letting ourselves off the hook from taking responsibility for our negative mindset when we repeat an affirmation of this kind?

Absolutely not. We are accepting what is and how we are in that moment without beating ourselves up about it or labeling ourselves in an outdated judgmental fashion. Beating ourselves up and over-identifying with a behaviour that isn't working for us, or for anyone else for that matter, is not how we will ultimately revolutionize our lives or our behaviour.

We must learn to accept ourselves *as we are:* the good, the bad, the ugly, the beautiful. Then, and only then, can we add both gentleness and assertiveness into the mix. We must be able to say, *"I love myself so I am willing to change that which I can change."*

It's easy to get comfortable with our old shoes, our old jokes, or our old ways of being and relating. There is nothing wrong or bad about familiarity, except that there is a whole lot more to life than becoming and allowing fixation in one area of our lives. Becoming fixed in only one way of being is not what life is about. Life's about flourishing and testing our limits. It's about setting our sights high and jumping over hurdles. Therefore, becoming increasingly aware of our behaviours by tempting them to reveal themselves through curious investigation utilizing neutralizing thoughts is a path to resetting our newer, updated lens through which we now view life.

Let's try a neutralizing thought on for size then. "Even though I myself have not been completely comfortable with my current circumstances, or in fact with change itself, I myself am comfortable with the idea of *entertaining* change and now begin to do so."

See how we both <u>announced the source of upset</u> *and* <u>separated ourselves from the need to judge or take immediate action</u>? Too often immediate action is *reaction* in emotional circumstances.

This neutrality is where the magic happens. We need to train our thoughts to neutralize rather than idealize, aimlessly hope, or worse yet, judge, which is the all-defeating, life-limiting, reaction.

Whatever you do, remember that a traumatic event (especially if it happened intentionally at the hands of another) can result in the loss of connection to the center of yourself, your natural breath, and your smile. So please remember to reclaim these while perusing all of the options you may choose to integrate into your life.

When you're making an observation about an event and/or the people involved try beginning with, "Whether or not I am correct, it does/doesn't *seem* like_____" (The blank is where you fill in your observation). Then, as you continue to complete your neutral thought finish the observation with, *"And, that's OK."* When we practice neutral thoughts we increase the workings of acceptance in our lives. This is the case whether they are spoken internally as part of our inner talk or spoken aloud. For example: *"Whether or not I am correct it doesn't seem like I'm going to get out of this appointment as early as I thought and that's OK."* By maintaining neutrality we bolster our confidence which in turn allows us act quicker and respond faster to challenging situations. Instead of reacting to my appointment running over I will respond with the best course of action I can think to take in that moment w*hile remaining calm, cool and collected.*

Finally, in a state of overwhelm, here is an effective neutral sentence for you to use: "I am flooded with emotion *and now I plan my next steps."*

A neutral mantra for resilience when dialoguing with ourselves is, *"I don't know how, but I know all of this is working out...and in my favour!"* That powerful affirmation has gotten me out of some tight spots! Faith in ourselves and faith in the unseen guiding power in our lives is where the awesomeness within our lives can and will expand *with practice.*

CHAPTER 42

How to Master Your Triggers

❦

LET'S FACE IT, HEADLINES IN the news are not always positive and this can trigger us to feel awful. The rational mind cannot always understand why certain events transpire that are of a brutal and violent nature.

One afternoon I felt particularly sad after reading about some traumatic events in the paper. This was one of those moments of being triggered. I had fallen prey to a journalist's agenda to only show her readers the shadow side of humanity and needed to make a positive shift by acknowledging that my curiosity had gotten the best of me and that it had been *my choice* to read those articles.

By making this acknowledgment I survived the feelings of helplessness and shifted from the state of victim to survivor in that moment. The news story with its inherent sadness was no longer holding me hostage because I could see the role that I myself had played in reacting to it.

Following that, a few seconds or a minute later, I decided that I would create an affirmation I could use from then on each and every time that I got sucked into dispiriting headlines. It goes like this:

"Fifteen million people kissed today for the first time. Fifteen million said I love you for the first time. At least 15 million took the first steps in following their dreams today. Fifteen million or more people got promoted today. Fifteen million people made the choice to embrace a new friendship today. Fifteen million people made the decision to embrace life today in some way, shape, or form that will bring them lasting happiness!"

WRITE A COMICAL STATEMENT

Looking at life from a new perspective is an almighty force. So, I invite you to take something that you've felt ashamed about and write a comical sentence in reference to it. Stash the line that you write in a drawer in the kitchen where you can easily find it and read it the next time you're feeling bothered by life in general, or by its details. Each and every time you pass by the hand scribbled note, even without a thought of changing anything about your day, you will subconsciously be *shifting* your perspective, *elevating* your spirit and *lifting* your vibrations.

Suggestion is all powerful when we are reprogramming our minds and *want* to change how we feel about certain things in our lives.

I will give you an example of how I've used this perspective-shifting tool in my life. When I was a kid I was often secretly embarrassed because of the way people reacted to my dad's age. Having an older father affected me in many ways. He was sixty-nine when I was born. His age was beneficial because of all the deep and varied life experience he had and all there was to learn from both him and his life stories. In other ways, I felt less comfortable about his age. In the short-term it was a challenge as a kid, but in the long run the implications of having an older father taught me many important life lessons. Like about embarrassment, for example. What *was* previously my childhood embarrassment taught me social autonomy in the long run and the strength of being *personally* resilient in the face of what other people may or may not think about me and my family.

Human beings thrive in greater capacities whenever there has been a hardship. We become mightier. Hence the adage: *"What doesn't kill you makes you stronger."*

Some friends' parents in our neighbourhood would not allow me and my siblings to spend too much time with their kids. Our parents were chastised for raising me to be "too free." I could do my homework *after* I ate dinner whereas other kids were required to do it as soon as they got home. I was allowed to bike and run around at the beach and in the neighborhood and forest, whereas they were not. I don't think either parenting style is right or wrong, but the effects of being ridiculed for my upbringing and the judgment around my dad's age were temporarily harmful and traumatizing to me.

One time I went to visit a friend in the neighbourhood. When I arrived at her front door, her mother (a woman who spent a lot of time home alone waiting on her husband to return, and was therefore generally a dissatisfied lady) said to me as she answered the door, "My daughter is not free to play. *She's* doing her homework." She leered at me as she said this, as if I should have been doing my homework right then, too. Then she said with scorn, "Wipe your face! You have dirt on it!" and shut the door in my face without saying another word.

I was only nine at the time and the ramification of her words stuck with me for years. Between that and having my siblings disparagingly taunt me by calling me "Daddy's Princess" and "Spot" for my eczema, I carried a sense for a long time that I was not deserving or good enough.

But good enough *for what*?

That's what I jokingly ask myself (and others) *now*. The idea is blasphemous that we ever question our capability in the first place...with *time, energy, awareness* of the interconnectedness of our existence, and *courage*, we literally *can* accomplish anything!

Life has all the ingredients. We just need to get cooking with them!

As I thought about how I might bring light to the old feelings of embarrassment and alienation from what is "normal" I recalled how nine out of ten grocery store checkout line girls would *oooo* and *ahhh*, "Awww... You got to go to the grocery store with your *granddad* today!" And, me curtly responding, "He's my Dad." one thing did come to mind. I meditated on the kitchen drawer scrap paper idea that I might put away for safekeeping for a rainy day.

Since my dad had been married five times before my mother (whom he was with for twenty-three years) and had more than a couple of children with those previous marriages before the girls in my immediate family were born I wrote the following:

> *"I applaud my father for his virility and ability to*
> *adapt to new circumstances."*

Lyrical, yes?

   . . .

Whether or not your own comical statement sounds lyrical is not of the essence. Write something that *sheds light* and *acceptance* on circumstances that might still be carried within you that formerly made you uncomfortable. It is the power of the human spirit *and mind* to turn potentially unfavourable circumstances into our personal gain.

I so enjoy reading that sticky note each time I reach for my spatula.

CHAPTER 43

The Effectiveness of Personal Agreements

જ્જ

A PERSONAL AGREEMENT IS A PROMISE we make to ourselves in order to heal from trauma. You'll know which ones to make when you consider how you and your life have been affected by trauma. Perhaps the most important personal agreement I have made is to take the free flow of my breath back.

I lost my connection with my breath at about eight years of age, on the day my half-brother died. When the doorbell rang, I was the one to greet the police officer at the door who came to the house bearing the shocking news. After I saw him, I ran up the stairs to tell my two sisters. I had overheard the officer asking my dad if he was the father of "Albert." In the moment, I was winded. Afterward my body remembered the sensation of lacking breath and associated it with fear. From that day forward, every time I got scared, my breath would become almost nonexistent, and anxiety would kick in. This was the case until I finally felt the sensation once again of having breath in all the places the body is meant to.

In 2003, when I was undergoing the prerequisites of my upcoming 2006 yoga teacher training, my teacher instructed me to put my hand over my stomach and feel my belly expand *with each inhalation,* like a baby's naturally does. Before then, I had thought the opposite: that I was meant to squeeze my belly with each inhalation. The phenomenon is that as babies we *know* how to breathe properly. The body's natural inclination is to expand on inhalation.

My yoga teacher's mere suggestion gave me back the sensation of my natural breath. Seeing as my brother died when I was eight and it took me until I was nineteen to feel a whole-body breath again, you can imagine the difference this made to my sense of overall well-being. I felt calm for the first time in a very long time!

I tell you this story because on that day I vowed to come in contact with my breath as quickly as possible in the future, despite feelings of fear, worry, strain, or stress in the moment. That personal agreement has enabled me to become calmer when I'm triggered. This personal agreement has changed *my life* and it has made it possible for me to take life-expanding, life-enriching, *and life-granting* risks again!

What personal agreements will you make?

Another of mine is to smile several times throughout the day. I put zero pressure on myself to change my state of being, my felt sense, or my emotional sense, however by smiling all of these aspects of who I am, including my physical sense of self, are made to feel lighter and I feel nourished by the mere act of doing so.

It's amazing what personal agreements can do for us. They enrich our connections to ourselves. They give us a sense of belonging within ourselves. They create the space for us to continue to grow on our individual paths and enliven the moments of our lives.

A colleague once asked me to supply my definition of success for a website. Upon reflection, I came up with the following statement, which I still appreciate a great deal.

> "Success is being able to think *when* I want to think, *how* I want to think, and *what* I want to think. Success is genuinely knowing that I have nothing to prove, and acting from that place."

So many people don't have this luxury because they fail to acknowledge that they *do* have it. It makes a difference to value your personal thoughts. My personal agreement to responsibly choose my thoughts, thus creating my own mental headspace, has emboldened me to live and love on after trauma. Perhaps it can do the same for you.

May your recovery from trauma bring you freedom and empowerment beyond measure.

Twelve Must-Dos for a Happy Life!

⌘

IF YOU DO THE FOLLOWING TWELVE THINGS ON A DAILY BASIS, you'll recover more quickly from the stress and aftereffects of trauma and be more resilient, calm, and even *joyful.* Mind, body, and spirit are interconnected. If you strengthen one, you are strengthened on every level. Photocopying and posting this list on your refrigerator is also a rewarding idea!

1. **Water** repairs cells, balances hormones, increases the levels of neurotransmitters like melatonin (supports restful sleep) and serotonin (builds happiness into our brains!) and more! So, drink a lot of water!

2. Taking at least a ten-minute **stroll** at lunchtime improves digestion and the assimilation of nutrients. As you walk, take lower belly breaths. Taking two or three of these ten-minute walks a day outdoors creates long, lean muscles and improves our moods, as walking outdoors connects us to the same life force that supports, feeds, and clothes us. Because of this, our immunity is strengthened.

3. Have you ever heard someone say "You are what you eat" or as the great Einstein is quoted, "Food is sunlight condensed into matter"? These ideas ring true to me! If you want to have boundless energy, **eat 75 per cent foods grown under the sun.** Sunlight helps our bodies to metabolize certain building blocks that we

need to stay healthy. This advice is especially important for those living in damper, wetter climates.

4. If you can **buy foods without chemicals,** your body will have more energy to do the activities you LOVE to do rather than for reversing the toxic effects of chemicals you've eaten. Chemicals that are commonly found in food include pesticides, preservatives, additives, colorings, synthetic growth hormones, and antibiotics.

5. Make a concerted effort upon waking up to create a thought that is centered on something that you look forward to that day. Then **give gratitude** for whatever it is.

6. **Give gifts, compliments, and appreciation freely,** without being asked or prompted, and in this way spread light through your environment.

7. **Discover yourself** outside of your many roles: Periodically throughout the day, stop for a moment and take a few deep breaths with your eyes closed. This will help to find that special someone who you are outside of the titles you have been assigned and the roles you are playing!

8. **Remember your humanity.** At the time of birth, each of us was a human being, before we became a human doing. It is from this *beingness* that we can still derive our strength and generate a greater supply of energy!

9. Watch what you put in your mind; **be careful of the information you ingest**. The media often highlight tragedy, for instance, and you may not wish to stimulate your nervous system with these kinds of images, which can be triggering. As much as it's important to know what's happening in the world, it's also important to return to the blessings in our own personal lives and communities. The most important reality is within.

10. **Initiate hugs.** Touch is essential if we are to foster connection to the truth that at the end of the day we are all one!

11. If our habits form who we are, then take time to **stretch beyond your norm.** Do something that really lights you up. *Take*

a chance . . . or just a moment to come back to the pure, ageless example of spirit within.

12. Make only one practice routine: instant forgiveness. **Forgive as fast as possible,** each and every time you feel you've been harmed in any degree. You are the powerhouse of your own life, which means that only you can ignite the sparks of a new life or touch on vaster experience with a single choice. Instant freedom through forgiveness is everyone's birthright.

Epilogue

❧

THE ULTIMATE SOLUTION FOR THE PAIN OF TRAUMA IS TO BECOME GREATER THAN YOU WERE BEFORE THE EVENT. The key is to take the strengths you discover and use them to build a life of purpose that gives you happiness.

It is known by many that the hippocampus and amygdala are survival centers in the brain that have the capacity to make choices without the participation of your conscious, willful mind when they sense that you are under threat. Your body can freeze as a direct result of this brain mechanism, and if it does, in that moment when you don't know if you'll ever be able to move again, you must make a conscious choice to have movement in your life. Moving forward is a key aspect of healing. It's the ultimate solution to the aftereffects of trauma and trauma drama.

If a human being throws choice out the window for you against your will at any point in time, then it must become a decision that you make *to redeem choice itself* and make it your number one ally moving forward.

After my rape, I felt ashamed and cut off from my community. I was part of a statistic I had never thought I would be included in. I didn't want the people around me to pity me because of my trauma. At the same time, I felt like I was developing new depths of being. I was scared of the depth of my experience and didn't know how to weave what was going on for me into my ordinary life and daily routines; in fact, I didn't know how I was going to be happy again. Have you felt the same way because of a trauma that you experienced? Whatever it was? Have you ever known anyone who has felt this way?

Fortunately the shame was temporary. I soon realized that the best way to ensure my recovery was to return to the great force that is community. Community in context to the survivor is any group of people who are working toward not only being the best version of themselves but helping others be the greatest version of themselves, too! Thinking outside of ourselves, considering others, as a survivor of any major life trauma, is the key to joining the flow of life again, and trusting.

Join the community(ies) that make the most heartfelt sense to you, *in relation to your own individual healing path.*

If you've experienced abuse, whether it be psychological, physical and/or sexual, the title *survivor* is the gift you receive for no longer being a victim of other people's actions. Although this is the case, it might also be challenging to go about life as you always have, for much of what you have known in your life has now changed. Being a survivor at times may seem like your greatest weakness because you can get triggered at the most unpredictable of times. At times, concern for your very survival poses your greatest challenge, because the survivor in you doesn't want the past to repeat. Nonetheless, I have learned that after a traumatic event, *knowing* you are a survivor is where your greatest strength lies. It is the pulse that keeps you awake in this moment. The awareness that you are someone who has already overcome so much.

You must recognize that you need to become more than you ever were in the past in order to thrive in the future. Reclaiming yourself in all your fullness is the key to thriving. You may wish to imagine you are seeing yourself for the first time, from the perspective of someone who has overcome something that once seemed greater than she or he was.

To see yourself as someone *strong* and capable like this takes work.

And, plenty of love.

Our emotional needs as survivors of trauma may cause us to place demands on the people around us. When our wounds are most fresh, asking those people to love and nurture us to *great* extents, while they at the same time try to meet the demands of their own daily needs, can present more of a challenge than is otherwise necessary.

For survivors, it is vital to remember that there are experts who are waiting to be of assistance to you and the direction of your unique healing path. Coaches, psychologists, authors giving inspirational and helpful seminars, classes and workshops locally AND around the world enthusiastically wait to assist you.

For friends of survivors, remember that survivors of trauma hope that their loved ones will be able to intuitively sense what they need in order to heal. Survivors have an immense desire to be supported on their journey of healing, even when they themselves may say that they do not want any help. Often knowing someone cares is enough.

The journey to rebuild a life and regain your positive sense of self after surviving a trauma is not always easy. It's also not easy to watch someone struggle to do so. Even when our aim clearly is to love another person, we cannot always make the mark from the recipient's point of view. Everyone has a different perception of what exactly love is and isn't. During recovery from trauma, forgiveness must be coupled with love. We must forgive ourselves for not always knowing how to help our loved ones or ourselves. We must also forgive those who do not always care for us in the way that we desire.

As survivors, we must learn how to let go when others do not meet our definition of what love is, and what it isn't.

Love looks like different things at different times on different days.

This is why I now share my vision is to create a haven for survivors called the Viva Standing Foundation. The Foundation prides itself on its vision of delivering excellent services to promote personal well-being and resilience after trauma, such as how to empower oneself post-trauma with new thoughts, restructuring one's chosen environments, fostering new and deepened relationships, growing healthy body connection and guiding survivors through much needed emotional healing. The proceeds from these book sales go to the purchase of a housing structure for The Viva Standing Foundation where survivors of trauma engage in a three and six month program to rebuild their inner and outer lives through community and learning to engage self-care principles. The house will promote wellness in the willing and voluntary participants, and reacquaint them with how to be a steward of the most positive mind-set possible, a vibrant body, self-empowerment, and self-mastery.

The objective is for the survivors to believe that they have a purpose, and to see and realize their place in the world *as they are today* by the time the program closes.

The Foundation is building a transformation house for participants who voluntarily opt to enrich their lives for the set time of the program. This is not a shelter for victims of abuse, as many are, but rather a place for survivors to learn to thrive in their lives emotionally, mentally, physically and spiritually with the help and support of community.

Thank you for purchasing this book.

Acknowledgments

❧

THE PEOPLE WHO HAVE STOOD by me over the last decade are diamonds in the rough. Thank you to each and every one of my loyal friends around this sacred planet. Thank you to the kindred of spirit: the yogis, artists, travelers, seekers, and open-hearted souls who entertained my whims and contemplated my pontifications. You gave me courage to go on. All aspects of life have been made rich because of your *presence*. My special thanks goes to:

To Jules Ginocchio, in Kentucky, who took a risk by turning her business over to my neophyte teaching skills in 2005.

To Melinda for agreeing to lead my first online program with me.

To my mother, for giving me her every Saturday morning as we read the first draft of my first book together in 2008 sitting in our entirely separate countries.

To Ren Jones for reminding me of the red carpet and the "glow" from living on purpose.

To Sujith Ravindran and all guests on the *Heal Your Trauma Drama* 2014 show.

To Steve Harrison of The Quantum Leap Program in Philadelphia, PA.

To each of my coaching clients and students over the years. Thank you.

To my Dad, for being an unstoppable adventurer and entrepreneurial optimist.

To *Maya the Wonder Dog,* World's Best Hiking Companion.

To Stephanie Gunning the editor of this book.

And, to Lane Yeatman Malbon for showing me that real men cry.

Resources

༄

OURVETCOMMUNITY.COM

OUR MISSION IS TO BRING love, light, laughter and healing to America's Armed Forces. Learn self-regulation and self-soothing techniques from certified coaches, experienced teachers from around the world, health professionals certified in various modalities and upstanding people who have walked the line and come out the other side. **PLUS:** Get all of Jo's full-length dance and yoga videos… You may Opt-In for a 30-Day Virtual Pass from wherever you are in the world! This membership is available for both retired and active duty military. **Website:** www.OurVetCommunity.com.

THE VIVA STANDING FOUNDATION

The Viva Standing Foundation was established to improve the lives of people who have experienced rape and/or war by offering community and tools of healing and personal empowerment in order to bring new-found meaning and purpose to the lives of survivors.

Website: www.vivastanding.org

CONNECT WITH JO STANDING

* **Website:** www.JoStanding.com
* **Facebook:** www.facebook.com/viva.standing

- **LinkedIn:** https://www.linkedin.com/in/jostanding/
- **Instagram:** www.instagram.com/jo.standing

Do you live in Canada, the USA, United Kingdom, Australia, New Zealand, Indonesia, Europe or Hong Kong? If yes, request to book Jo Standing to speak to your group on trauma resilience this year!

You may email vivastanding@gmail.com for more information.

ONLINE VIDEOS TO WATCH

The Biology of Belief by Bruce Lipton
So Much Magnificence by Deva Premal and Mitten
Power Healing Theta Meditation—528 hzs YouTube Video
The Power of Vulnerability by Brene Brown
The Mask You Live In by The Representation Project and Team

RECOMMENDED BOOKS

Acupressure for Emotional Healing by Beth Ann Henning and Michael Reed Gach, Ph.D.
After the Ecstasy, the Laundry Jack Kornfield
The Art of Conscious Loving by Charles and Caroline Muir
The Art of Traditional Thai Massage by Asokananda (Harald Brust)
Ask and It Is Given by Esther and Jerry Hicks
Authentic Happiness by Martin Seligman

Chakra Tonics by Elise Marie Collins
Fly, My Love, Fly by Tina Robinson-Robinson
Heal Your Body A-Z by Louise Hay
Heal Your Life by Louise Hay
How Can I Help? by Ram Dass and Paul Gorman
How to Win Friends and Influence People by Dale Carnegie
Inward Revolution by J. Krishnamurti
The Magic of Believing by Claude M. Bristol
Overcoming Trauma Through Yoga by David Emerson and Elizabeth Hopper Ph.D.
The Entrepreneur's Solution by Mel Abraham
The Pilates Body by Brooke Siler (A great guide for initial reconnection to the body.)
The Post-Traumatic Stress Disorder Sourcebook by Glenn R. Schiraldi, Ph.D.

The Power of Intention by Wayne Dyer
Think and Grow Rich by Napolean Hill
Timebound Traveler by David Newman
Quantum Wellness by Kathy Freston
Shantaram by Gregory David Roberts
Siddhartha by Hermann Hesse
Waking the Tiger by Peter Levine
War by Robert Greene
The War of Art: Break Through the Blocks and Win Your Inner Creative Battles
by Steven Pressfield

You Can Heal Your Life by Louise Hay

END NOTES

1. Daniel Amen, *Introduction*, http://danielamenmd.amenclinics.com/brain-scans-can-tell-traumatic-brain-injury-and-post-traumatic-stress-disorder-apart/

2. National Institutes of Health (NIH), *Introduction*, http://www.nimh.nih.gov/health/publications/post-traumatic-stress-disorder-easy-to-read/index.shtml

3. Mother Jones, *Introduction*, http://www.motherjones.com/politics/2013/01/charts-us-veterans-ptsd-war-iraq-afghanistan

4. Recognize Trauma, *Introduction*, http://www.recognizetrauma.org/statistics.php

5. National Trauma Institute, *Introduction*, http://www.nationaltrauma institute.org/home/trauma_statistics.html

6. Scientific American Magazine, *Introduction*, article, "Accidental Genius by Darold A. Treffert August 1, 2014

7. YouTube, *Introduction*, delta brainwave video, "8 Hour Deep Sleep Music: Delta Waves, Relaxing Music Sleep, Sleeping Music, Sleep Meditation ☯159" by the YellowBrickCinema channel.

8. The American Psychological Association, *Chapter One*, http://www.apa.org/topics/trauma/

9. Thich Nhat Hanh, *Chapter Four*, "Living Buddha, Living Christ"

10. Brene Brown, *Chapter Ten*, *The Power of Vulnerability* TED Talk online free video.

11. Dr. Emoto, *Chapter Thirty-Four*, Research on the effect of words, http://www.masaru-emoto.net/english/water-crystal.html

12. Yoga Journal, *Chapter Thirty-Four*, Mountain Pose Description, http://www.yogajournal.com/pose/mountain-pose/

13. Washington, DC Drop in Crime Study, Chapter Thirty-Six, http://www.worldpeacegroup.org/washington_crime_study.html

14. Ho'oponopono Clearing Meditation from Hawaii, Chapter Thirty-Six, http://www.thereisaway.org/Ho'oponopono_cleaning_meditation.htm

15. BlogTalk Radio, Chapter Thirty-Nine, free resource for creation of affirmation MP3s, www.blogtalkradio.com

About the Author

❧

AMERICAN-BORN AUTHOR JO STANDING RETURNED to the USA following almost 10 years of living in Vancouver, Canada, and traveling abroad to Europe, Australia and Asia. She taught wellness and empowerment classes to the public for 8 of the 10 years. Since returning, Jo has been given the blessing of sharing her journeys with Americans through her article and book writing, her speaking, and social media, as well as at *The Harvard Faculty Club*. She is the praised author of *Conquer Trauma Drama: Get Your Life Back* published in 2015. In 2016 and 2017, she wrote the follow-up *Conquer Trauma Drama: Breakthrough Curriculum* that can be worked through in tandem with the paperback. Jo has had the honor of having her writing featured in USA TODAY, Elephant Journal, and Huff Post, as interviewed by Dr. Felicia Clark. She is a life-long student and has the honor of studying with doctors who come from a long lineage of holistic studies.

Jo began OurVetCommunity.com an online community as she is the daughter of a deceased Army man who struggled with the aftereffects of war long after his involvement ended. She prides herself as being a *"Daddy's Girl,"* and wants all daughters to feel safe and loved around their daddies and mommies when they return home from Service. It is because of this that she works to serve veterans during their transition, as they learn to return home to their personal selves again. She also looks back fondly on her visits to Richmond, Virginia to see her late Great Uncle Doug Davis who was a Captain in the U.S. Navy, and an interpreter more than once for the late President John F. Kennedy.

www.ingramcontent.com/pod-product-compliance
Lightning Source LLC
LaVergne TN
LVHW011218080426
835509LV00005B/199